MICROWAVE
COOKING
STEP BY STEP

EDITED BY
ANNE MARSHALL

 BayBooks

An imprint of HarperCollins*Publishers*

STOCKISTS

Accoutrement Cook Shop
611 Military Road
Mosman NSW
Tel: (02) 969 1031
(also Lemongrove, Chatswood)

The Bay Tree
40 Holdsworth Street
Woollahra NSW
Tel: (02) 328 1101

Janet Niven Antiques
118 Queen Street
Woollahra NSW
Tel: (02) 363 2211

Villa Italiana
566 Military Road
Mosman NSW
Tel: (02) 960 1788

A BAY BOOKS PUBLICATION
Bay Books, an imprint of
HarperCollins*Publishers*
25 Ryde Road, Pymble, Sydney NSW 2073, Australia
31 View Road, Glenfield, Auckland 10, New Zealand

First published in Australia in 1993

National Library of Australia
Cataloguing-in-Publication data:
    Marshall, Anne, 1938- .
        Microwave step-by-step.
        Includes index.
        ISBN 1 86378 022 X.
        1. Microwave cookery. I. Title. (Series: Bay Books cookery collection).
    641.5882

Food Stylist on cover and double spreads Anne Marshall
Food Stylist's Assistant Ann Bollard
Front cover and double spread photographs by Quentin Bacon
Front cover recipe: Chicken and Eggplant Cacciatore (page 44)
Back cover recipe: Apple and Berry Crumble (page 88)
Other photographs by Ashley Barber
Recipes by Anne Marshall, Douglas Marsland and Jan Rudd
Styling by Voula Mantzouridis and Jan Rudd
Charts and Information reprinted from:
Australian Meat and Live-Stock Corporation
Fish Marketing Authority

Printed by Griffin Press, Adelaide
Printed in Australia

9 8 7 6 5 4 3 2 1
96 95 94 93

CONTENTS

Microscape Know How

A re you getting the most out of your microwave or are you only using it for defrosting and reheating food and making cups of coffee? This collection of recipes will inspire you to use it more often. Foods are featured that cook exceptionally well in a microwave; vegetables, fish and chicken in particular. Many of the recipes have step-by-step photographs which take you with ease through the preparations. The range is from basic to classic, trendy to healthy and all save you time because they can be cooked quickly, without fuss. There are pasta and rice dishes, speedy snacks for today's hectic lifestyle and surprising desserts, chocolates and cakes for those with a sweet tooth. A delicious collection for all ages and all occasions — even confident microwave users will love them!

BEFORE YOU BEGIN

Check Watts and Times!
Microwave ovens differ in the power output from 500–750 W (at the time of writing). A magnetron is rated in watts, just like a light bulb. A magnetron is a special tube in a microwave oven which converts electricity to microwaves. The higher the wattage, the faster the food will cook. A high wattage also indicates a larger oven.

When using microwave recipes, or following microwave pack instructions, it is most important to check the power level in watts of your microwave oven and relate these to times and instructions given, adjusting if necessary, for the best results. The wattage is given either on the front of the door or on the door lining or at the back of the microwave oven.

All cooking times given in the following recipes are approximate. However, the recipes were prepared and tested in 600 and 650 watt microwave ovens and the times given are based on these. If you have a more powerful 750 watt oven, you will need to reduce times by a minute or two; if yours is a smaller 500 watt oven, add a minute or two. Remember, undercooking can be easily rectified, overcooking can't.

Variable power levels and times can be selected in a microwave oven from dials or touch control panels. The dial settings are referred to in the recipes in this book. The following chart explains the relationship between dial settings and percentages of power.

The Advantages of Microwave Cooking

TIME Microwave cooking can save time. Superb meals for the family can be prepared in moments and meat left in the freezer can be taken out and quickly defrosted.

ECONOMY Microwave cooking uses less energy. The energy output is less than a conventional oven and therefore it consumes less power. Foods cook faster and there's no preheating unless you are using the browning dish. Savings in energy and time mean savings with the power bill.

CONVENIENCE Defrosting, reheating and shorter cooking times make the microwave oven ideal for today's busy lifestyle. Meals can be prepared, cooked, frozen and reheated all in the same dish, then served piping hot.

NUTRITION Microwave ovens don't boil all the goodness away. The speed of cooking plus the small amount of liquid required means

Microwave Heat	Power %	Cooking Purpose
High	90–100%	Boil, grill
Medium High	70–80%	Roast, reheat
Medium	50–60%	Poach, bake
Low	30–40%	Simmer
Defrost	30–35%	Defrost
Warm	10–20%	Warm

super-nutritious meals. Vegetables retain their vitamins and minerals. In addition, the colour of cooked vegetables is excellent and food presentation is thus enhanced. For many people the microwave is worthwhile just for cooking vegetables.

DIET Nutritious, low calorie foods can be ready in minutes and the temptation to reach for fattening snacks while waiting for dinner is greatly reduced.

COOL COOKING The microwave is particularly useful during the hot summer months. No more slaving over a hot stove or in a steam-filled kitchen because microwave ovens do not generate heat. All the energy produced is absorbed by the food and the kitchen remains cool and comfortable.

QUICK CLEANUPS Food does not stick or bake on to casserole dishes in the microwave, which makes cleaning up much easier. Because fewer dishes are used (one dish can go from freezer to oven to table) there's often less washing up. Microwave dishes may be washed in a dishwasher which saves time and contributes to smoother running of the household. The ovens themselves just need a quick wipeover to clean.

What are Microwaves?

A microwave is an electromagnetic wave within a particular frequency band. It is similar to electromagnetic waves found in radio, light and heatwaves. A microwave is generated by electricity passing through a special vacuum tube called a magnetron. Microwaves are short (hence the name 'micro'), high frequency waves which travel in virtually straight lines and can be reflected, transmitted and absorbed. It is these special qualities which enable them to be used in ovens to cook food.

The Microwave Oven

Microwave ovens take advantage of microwave energy by trapping the waves which are then absorbed by the food. Once absorbed, the energy is converted into heat.

When you switch on the power, electricity is converted to microwaves by a magnetron — the heart of the microwave oven. (This only produces microwaves when the oven is switched on, the door properly shut and the timer set.) A wave guide directs the microwaves into the oven cavity. As the waves don't penetrate metal they bounce off the metal of the interior walls and the fine mesh door screen, penetrating the food from all angles. With some models the waves are distributed by a fan-like stirrer, while others have a turntable which rotates the food through either 180° or 360°. Some models combine these features.

Microwave cooking offers an exciting new approach to food preparation. You can cook and serve meals in the same dish, or cook and eat off the one plate. China, paper, plastic and heat-resistant glass can all be used for cooking or reheating in the microwave oven. Recipes are different, too. Times are shorter and less liquid is used.

In traditional conventional ovens the food slowly absorbs the

heat from the oven. The food gets hot and so does the kitchen and the cook. In microwave cookery, because the heat is inside the food, the kitchen stays cool, likewise the cook.

The microwaves penetrate the food from all angles causing the water and fat molecules to vibrate. This produces friction which creates the heat which cooks the food. Because the heat is inside the food, it keeps cooking once you take it out of the oven. Standing time is an important part of the technique of microwave cooking.

Microwaves are odourless and tasteless. No residue remains in the food at all. In fact microwaved meals can be especially delicious and nutritious because the food is cooked quickly with all the flavours retained — not boiled or baked away.

How Microwaves Cook Food

1 Microwaves are directed into the oven cavity by the wave guide.
2 The stirrer fan distributes the waves. Some models also have a turntable to rotate food while cooking.

Basic Equipment for Successful Microwave Cooking

Item	Use
20 x 20 cm (8 x 8 in) square dish	Cakes, slices, whole corn cobs, confectionery, vegetables, lasagne
Roasting and grilling rack	Pork, beef, lamb, veal, roasts, chicken, duck, turkey, bacon, sausages
Browning casserole dish	Grilling chops and steaks, stews, curries, casseroles, baking scones, frying seafood, crumbed foods, eggs
3 litre casserole with lid	Soups, pasta, rice, casseroles, corned beef, vegetables
Casserole lid	Pavlovas, pies, quiches, vegetables, omelettes, cheesecakes and for cooking small quantities of food
Ring dish	Baked custards, breads, scone rings, cakes, whole peeled potatoes
Ceramic flan dish	Cheesecakes, fruit flans, quiches, vegetables
Loaf dish	Meat loaves, loaf cakes, breads
Flat round platter	Fruit and savoury pizzas, vegetable platters, sweet and savoury biscuits, fruit flambé
Various sized basins	Melting, blanching
1 or 2 litre (32 or 64 fl oz) jugs	Sauces, custards, reheating
Soufflé dish casseroles	Round cakes, soufflés, puddings, reheating soups,
White kitchen paper towels (not recycled)	Reheating cakes and breads, lining dishes and to cover food to prevent splatters
Plastic wrap and bags	Use recognised brand names for covering food when no lid is available, for steaming vegetables and seafood
Aluminium foil	As long as the density of the food is greater than the amount of foil, foil can be used on the edges of roasts, cakes and drumsticks. During standing time partially cover roasts so that heat is retained. Foil lining can also be used to prevent the sides of a fruit cake from drying. Use foil to cover the cooked portion of a cake when the centre is still moist

3 Microwaves cannot penetrate metal, so are randomly deflected off oven walls. This promotes even cooking.

4 The waves penetrate the food to a depth of about 5 cm (2 in).

5 They produce friction which creates heat which cooks the food.

6 Heat spreads to the centre by conduction. Stirring food or turning it encourages even cooking.

Which Dish?

MICROWAVE-SAFE COOKWARE
There's no need to rush out and buy special cookware for your microwave oven. The kitchen cupboard is probably full of bowls and casserole dishes which are ideal — Pyrex, Corning-ware, china bowls and plates for example. Even ordinary items such as paper or plastic plates, wooden or wicker baskets can be used if you just want to warm food.

Converting Conventional Recipes for Microwave Cooking

Only choose conventional recipes that will make, at most 6 to 8 servings. Recipes yielding large quantities will not effectively use the convenience of microwave cooking.

Select recipes which use ingredients with high natural moisture levels such as poultry, minced meats, vegetables, fish, fruits and sauces.

When you have found a recipe you wish to convert, find a similar microwave recipe and use it as a guide.

The Basic Conversion Steps

1 Always cut meat and vegetables into the same sized pieces for casseroling and steaming.

2 Reduce liquid by one-third to one-half when converting recipes for microwave preparation as liquid attracts microwave energy and slows the cooking of other ingredients. If necessary add extra liquid towards the end of cooking.

3 Reduce salt by two-thirds for microwave cooking and adjust other seasonings before serving. Microwave cooking enhances the natural flavour of foods therefore conventional recipes can be over-seasoned.

4 Add delicate ingredients such as shellfish, cheese, canned and fine cooked foods near the end of cooking to prevent toughening by overcooking.

5 Reduce fats and oils which have been included in conventional cooking to prevent sticking. Add fats and oils only for their flavour qualities.

6 Reduce liquids in cakes by 2 tablespoons and replace with an extra egg.

7 Sauces which contain cream, sour cream, yoghurt or moist cheese are cooked and then reheated on medium.

8 Thin liquids such as water, fruit juices, stock, wine and the natural juices of canned vegetables can be heated on high.

9 Major ingredients like poultry, whole fish fillets and minced or cubed meats can be microwaved on high until hot, then on medium to avoid overcooking. Stir microwave cooked foods that are stirred in conventional cookery.

10 Foods that cannot be stirred should be cooked on medium and the dish rotated four times during cooking if there is no turntable.

11 Cakes are best cooked on medium and finished on high for the last 2 to 3 minutes.

12 Soups, casseroles and roasts are best started on high for the first 5 minutes and finished on medium.

Reheating Techniques and Principles

ELEVATE   Large cooked dishes (ie lasagne or meatloaf) should be elevated to ensure even reheating.

COVER   Covering not only ensures cooked meals do not dry out, it speeds reheating time.

STIR   Stirring cooked dishes distributes heat evenly.

ROTATE   Rotate cooked dishes that cannot be stirred, eg lasagne.

SHIELDING   Shield edges of cooked dishes (eg lasagne or meat loaves) with foil to prevent edges overcooking.

STANDING   Allow a few minutes standing time before serving large dishes.

ARRANGEMENT   If reheating a plated meal, arrange food so that items which take longer to heat are round the outside of the plate, ie meat on the outside, vegetables in the centre.

STARTING TEMPERATURE   A cooked dish, chilled for a short time, will reheat quicker than a dish that has been refrigerated all day.

- Fat attracts more microwave energy than meat, so trim meat of any fat before freezing to ensure even defrosting.

- Before defrosting meat, remove freezer bag or wrap to prevent meat sitting in 'drip' which will otherwise boil, causing defrosting meat to 'stew'.

- To remove frozen meat from freezer wrap or bag, defrost for a few mintues until the wrap or bag is easily removed. Remove metal twist ties from bags to prevent arcing.

- If meat is purchased frozen on a styro-foam tray, remove from tray before defrosting. Styro-foam trays are not microwave-safe.

- When freezing cooked meals, always keep in mind the suitability of the dish for microwave defrosting and reheating (ie shape and whether the material is both freezer- and microwave-safe).

- Meals frozen in foil containers can be defrosted and reheated in the microwave oven, providing the container is no more than 4 cm (1 ½ in) deep and the foil lid is removed.

- Best results are achieved if reheating individual portions of a cooked dish rather than the whole cooked dish, eg slices of lasagne or meatloaf, which is faster and gives a more even result.

- Pre-browned steaks, chops and patties may be reheated without defrosting.

- Reheating times for pre-browned steaks etc will vary according to required taste, thickness, and degree of cooking when initially browned.

A Vegetable Feast

*T*he microwave oven cooks vegetables very well — they retain their natural appetising colour and have an appealing *al dente* or slightly crisp texture while retaining vitamins and minerals. The flavoursome vegetable recipes that follow are guaranteed to brighten up a meal and win you some compliments.

Layer sliced potatoes in shallow dish

Combine celery, basil, stock, olive oil, vinegar and pepper

Pour sauce over potatoes before serving

Recipes on previous pages: Vegetable Stir Fry (page 21), Stuffed Golden Nugget Pumpkins (page 16)

Potato Salad with Bacon

POTATO SALAD WITH BACON

TIME: 17 MINUTES
SERVES 6

6 medium-sized potatoes, peeled and thinly sliced

1 stalk celery, chopped

½ teaspoon dried basil

½ cup (125 ml/4 fl oz) chicken or vegetable stock

1 tablespoon olive oil

3 tablespoons white vinegar

freshly ground black pepper

60 g (2 oz) smoked bacon, diced and cooked

1 Place sliced potatoes in a shallow dish. Cover and cook on high 10 to 12 minutes. Set aside.

2 Combine celery, basil, stock, olive oil, vinegar and pepper in a 4 cup (1 litre/32 fl oz) measure. Cook on high 5 minutes then add bacon.

3 Pour over potatoes and serve warm.

Serve with veal or chicken.

GADO GADO SALAD

TIME: 8 MINUTES

SERVES 8

500 g (1 lb) bean sprouts or shoots

250 g (8 oz) finely shredded cabbage

250 g (8 oz) green beans, cut in 2 cm (¾ in) lengths

2 large carrots, cut matchstick size

SAUCE

1 onion, sliced

2 cloves garlic, chopped

2 teaspoons oil

¼ teaspoon salt

2 teaspoons brown sugar

1 teaspoon fresh lemon juice

1 teaspoon soy sauce

Gado Gado Salad

1 teaspoon chilli sauce

125 g (4 oz) crunchy peanut butter

½ cup (125 ml/4 fl oz) coconut milk

GARNISH

sliced cucumber

sliced radish

sliced hard-boiled egg

parsley sprigs

1 Place bean sprouts, cabbage, beans and carrots into individual plastic bags with 1 tablespoon water for each bag. Fold in open edge. Place bags in microwave oven and cook on high 3 to 4 minutes until vegetables are crispy tender. Rinse vegetables in cold water and drain.

2 To make sauce, place onion, garlic and oil in a microwave safe bowl. Cook on high 5 minutes. Add remaining sauce ingredients and blend well.

3 Place peanut sauce in a serving bowl. Arrange blanched vegetables on a flat salad platter. Garnish with cucumber, radish, egg and parsley.

Chill and serve with an Asian-style meal.

COCONUT MILK

¾ cup (180 ml/6 fl oz) cold water

3 to 4 tablespoons desiccated coconut

Place water and coconut in a microwave safe bowl. Cover with plastic wrap and cook on high 2½ minutes. Allow to cool, strain and squeeze coconut with fingers.

BROCCOLI SALAD

TIME: 6 MINUTES
SERVES 6 TO 8

> 750 g (1½ lb) fresh broccoli
>
> 3 hard-boiled eggs, chopped
>
> 90 g (3 oz) dried red pimiento or capsicum (pepper), finely diced
>
> 10 black olives, stoned and chopped

ITALIAN DRESSING

> ¼ cup (60 ml/2 fl oz) olive oil
>
> 2 tablespoons strained fresh lemon juice
>
> 1 teaspoon grated lemon zest
>
> salt to taste
>
> ½ teaspoon dried oregano
>
> 1 clove garlic, finely chopped
>
> 1 tablespoon grated Parmesan cheese
>
> ½ teaspoon freshly ground pepper

1 Prepare broccoli by cutting into florets. Place into plastic bag with 1 tablespoon water and fold in open edge. Cook in microwave oven on high 5 to 6 minutes. Plunge broccoli in chilled water and drain well.

2 Arrange broccoli on a flat salad platter. Moisten with Italian dressing.

3 Sprinkle with chopped eggs, pimiento or capsicum and olives.

4 To make dressing, combine all ingredients, mix well and chill. Store in an airtight container. Mix again before using.

Serve with crisp bread rolls and a green salad or as part of a buffet party menu.

SALAD NICOISE

Broccoli Salad

TIME: 9 MINUTES
SERVES 6 TO 8

> 250 g (8 oz) green beans
>
> 3 medium-sized potatoes, peeled and diced
>
> 250 g (8 oz) tomatoes, chopped
>
> 1 tablespoon stuffed olives
>
> 15 g (½ oz) anchovy fillets
>
> 1 teaspoon capers
>
> 4 tablespoons vinaigrette dressing

1 Cut beans into 2.5 cm (1 in) pieces. Blanch for 2 minutes on high in a small casserole dish with 2 tablespoons water.

2 Place the potatoes in a bowl, cover with plastic wrap and cook on high 7 minutes. Set beans and potatoes aside to cool.

3 Toss potatoes, beans, tomatoes and olives together in a serving bowl. Combine anchovy fillets, capers and vinaigrette dressing. Pour over the vegetables and toss.

Serve chilled with crisp bread rolls for a light, hot weather meal.

GREEN AND WHITE SALAD

T I M E : 7 M I N U T E S
S E R V E S 8

  ½ small head cauliflower

  1 head fresh green lettuce

  ½ bunch curly endive

  250 g (8 oz) can artichoke hearts,
  drained

  12 black olives

D R E S S I N G

  ¼ cup (60 ml/2 fl oz) salad oil

  2 tablespoons tarragon or white
  vinegar

  ½ teaspoon salt

  1 clove garlic, crushed

1 Cut cauliflower into small florets each with a portion of stalk. Wash in cold water. Place into casserole dish and add 1 to 2 tablespoons cold water. Cover and cook on high 6 to 7 minutes until crispy tender. Rinse cauliflower in iced water to prevent overcooking.

2 Wash lettuce and endive and separate leaves from stalk. Refrigerate until crisp. Tear greens into bite-sized pieces and dry by shaking in a clean teatowel.

3 Place greens into glass salad bowl, cut artichokes into quarters and add to bowl with olives and cauliflower. Refrigerate until serving time.

4 Place dressing ingredients in a screw-top jar and shake well. Just before serving, add to salad and toss until vegetables are well coated.

Serve with cold sliced fillet of beef or as part of a buffet party menu.

U S I N G P L A S T I C B A G S

Plastic bags may be used for cooking vegetables. Twist neck and fold under to seal, or secure with an elastic band. Prick once or twice to allow hot air to escape during cooking.

VINAIGRETTE DRESSING

  3 tablespoons olive oil

  1 teaspoon French mustard

  1 tablespoon white or tarragon
  vinegar

  salt and ground pepper to taste

  1 clove garlic, crushed

1 Combine all ingredients in a jar. Replace lid and shake well. Store in an airtight jar in the refrigerator.

V A R I A T I O N S

English mustard (in place of French mustard)

chopped chives or parsley

chopped hard-boiled egg

strained fresh lemon juice (in place of vinegar)

Salad Nicoise

ASPARAGUS SAUCE

TIME: 2 MINUTES
SERVES 2

>   340 g (11 oz) can green
>   asparagus spears
>
>   ¾ cup (180 ml/6 fl oz) chicken
>   stock
>
>   salt and pepper
>
>   1 tablespoon cream

1   Combine asparagus with stock,
salt, pepper and cream. Purée in a
blender until smooth. Correct
seasonings.

2   Pour into a glass jug. Cook on
high 2 minutes.

Serve sauce with grilled or barbecued
fish.

HONEY GLAZED CARROTS

TIME: 8½ MINUTES
SERVES 4

>   500 g (1 lb) carrots, cut into
>   strips

HONEY SAUCE

>   15 g (½ oz) butter
>
>   2 tablespoons honey
>
>   2 tablespoons vinegar
>
>   2 tablespoons orange juice
>
>   salt
>
>   2 teaspoons cornflour

1   Place carrots in a microwave-safe
casserole with 1 tablespoon water.
Cook covered on high 5 to 6
minutes, stirring halfway through
cooking, drain.

2   Combine all sauce ingredients in a
glass bowl and cook on high 1 minute,
stirring after 30 seconds. Pour over
carrots, cook 2 minutes to reheat.

Serve with roast chicken.

CELERY AND ALMOND SAUTÉ

TIME: 6 MINUTES
SERVES 6 TO 8

>   8 stalks celery, cut in diagonal
>   slices
>
>   ⅓ cup chopped spring onions
>   (shallots)
>
>   30 g (1 oz) butter
>
>   pinch garlic salt
>
>   pinch white pepper
>
>   ½ teaspoon sugar
>
>   toasted flaked almonds

1   In a 1 litre (32 fl oz) casserole
combine celery, spring onions,
butter, garlic salt and pepper.

2   Cover and cook on high
6 minutes or until crisp but still
tender, stirring in sugar and
toasted almonds after 3 minutes.

Serve with fish.

Celery and Almond Sauté

BEETROOT WITH DILL SAUCE

TIME: 20 MINUTES
SERVES 4 TO 6

>   500 g (1 lb) fresh medium size
>   beetroot
>
>   ½ teaspoon salt
>
>   ½ cup (125 ml/4 fl oz) water

DILL SAUCE

>   15 g (½ oz) butter
>
>   1 tablespoon plain (all purpose)
>   flour
>
>   ½ teaspoon onion salt
>
>   freshly ground pepper
>
>   ¼ teaspoon sugar
>
>   ¾ cup (180 ml/6 fl oz) milk
>
>   2 teaspoons chopped fresh dill

1   Wash beetroot and cut off stalks
4 cm (1½ in) above the bulb. Place
evenly apart in a 2 litre (64 fl oz)
casserole. Stir salt into water and
pour over beetroot. Cover and cook
on high 15 minutes, turning beetroot
over halfway through cooking. Let
stand, covered, 5 minutes.

2 To make sauce, heat butter in a small bowl on high 1 minute. Stir in flour, seasonings and sugar. Blend in milk. Cook on high 2 minutes or until thickened. Stir in chopped dill.

3 Remove tips, skin and root ends from beetroot and cut each bulb into quarters. Arrange in serving dish.

4 Pour sauce over beetroot, cover and cook on medium 2 to 3 minutes to reheat.

Serve with grilled fish or steak.

SCALLOPED SWEET POTATOES

T I M E   1 4   M I N U T E S
S E R V E S   6

  750 g (1½ lb) orange sweet
  potatoes, thinly sliced

  2 rashers bacon, diced and cooked

  2 tablespoons plain (all purpose)
  flour

  ½ teaspoon salt

  ½ cup spring onions (shallots),
  sliced

  2 cups (500 ml/16 fl oz) warm
  milk

  1 cup (125 g/4 oz) grated tasty
  cheese

Scalloped Sweet Potatoes

  grated nutmeg and paprika
  chopped parsley, to sprinkle

1 Combine all ingredients in a greased microwave-safe casserole. Cover and cook on high 14 minutes, stirring every 4 minutes.

2 Sprinkle with extra nutmeg, paprika and chopped parsley before serving.

Serve with baked ham or roast chicken or with a barbecue.

PRICKING VEGETABLES

Certain vegetables such as tomatoes, zucchini, baby squash and potatoes should be pierced with a skewer before cooking. This enables steam to escape during cooking and prevents the vegetables from splitting.

WRAP COOKED POTATOES IN FOIL

Wrap cooked jacket potatoes in foil after cooking. They will retain their heat for 30 minutes and leave the microwave oven free for other cooking.

TOASTING SESAME SEEDS

30 g (1 oz) butter
3 tablespoons sesame seeds
Place butter in a pie plate and cook on high 30 seconds. Stir in sesame seeds and cook on high 3 to 4 minutes, stirring every minute until golden. Drain on white paper towel.

BABY BUTTERED POTATOES

TIME: 12 MINUTES
SERVES 4 TO 6

> 500 g (1 lb) baby new potatoes, washed
> 60 g (2 oz) butter
> 2 tablespoons chopped parsley
> celery salt

1 Place potatoes, butter and parsley in a shallow dish. Cover with plastic wrap. Cook on high 12 minutes, stirring after 6 minutes.

2 Stand covered 5 minutes. Serve hot, sprinkled with celery salt.

Serve with roast meat or casseroles.

JACKET POTATOES

TIME: 11 MINUTES
SERVES 4

> 4 medium even-sized potatoes, unpeeled
> peanut oil
> butter
> 4 tablespoons sour cream
> 2 rashers bacon, diced and cooked
> chopped chives

1 Wash and prick potatoes, brush with oil and wrap in plastic food wrap. Place in a circle around edge of turntable and cook on high 5 minutes. Turn over and cook a further 6 minutes.

2 Remove wrap and cut a cross on top of each potato. Squeeze firmly so that the centre will pop up. Top with butter or sour cream, bacon and chives.

Serve with beef steak.

STUFFED GOLDEN NUGGET PUMPKINS

TIME: 16 MINUTES
SERVES 4

> 4 golden nugget pumpkins
> 8 spring onions (shallots), sliced
> 30 g (1 oz) butter
> 12 green beans, sliced
> 185 g (6 oz) cooked rice
> 1 large tomato, chopped
> 2 tablespoons ground almonds
> 2 tablespoons grated Parmesan cheese
> extra grated Parmesan cheese or toasted sesame seeds, to sprinkle

1 Slice tops off pumpkins, reserve. Chop any flesh from top opening (approximately ⅓ cup) and scoop out seeds and fibres with a metal spoon.

2 Place pumpkins on edge of microwave turntable positioned as 'north, south, east, west' and cook in microwave on high 5 minutes.

3 Cook spring onions and butter in a small covered bowl on high 2 minutes. Add reserved pumpkin, cover and cook 1 minute.

4 Cook beans in a plastic bag on high 2 minutes.

5 Mix together beans, spring onion mixture, rice, tomato, almonds and cheese. Spoon into pumpkin shells, sprinkle with extra cheese or sesame seeds and cover with reserved pumpkin tops. Cook on high for 6 minutes.

Serve with grilled chops or steak or as a light meal with garlic bread and salad.

Pierce each squash 5 times with a skewer

Heat butter, onion and garlic

Add squash, tomatoes, basil and seasoning

BABY SQUASH PROVENCAL

TIME: 10 MINUTES
SERVE 6 TO 8

> 500 g (1 lb) baby squash, even-sized
>
> 60 g (2 oz) butter
>
> 60 g (2 oz) onion, chopped or sliced
>
> 1 clove garlic, chopped
>
> 500 g (1 lb) tomatoes, chopped
>
> 1 tablespoon chopped fresh basil
>
> ⅛ teaspoon salt
>
> ⅛ teaspoon pepper
>
> chopped parsley, to garnish

1 Pierce each squash 5 times with a skewer. If large, cut into quarters.

2 Heat butter, onion and garlic on high 4 minutes in a medium-sized bowl covered with clear plastic wrap.

3 Add chopped tomatoes, basil, salt, pepper and squash. Cover and cook on high 5 to 6 minutes until squash is fork tender. Sprinkle with chopped parsley to serve.

Serve as an accompaniment to a main course.

Baby Squash Provencal

VEGETABLE LASAGNE

TIME: 24 MINUTES
SERVES 4 TO 6

- *250 g (8 oz) ricotta cheese*
- *125 g (4 oz) mozzarella cheese, grated*
- *2 teaspoons chopped parsley*
- *3 long zucchini*
- *2 large ripe tomatoes, sliced*
- *250 ml (8 fl oz) homemade tomato sauce (see recipe page 22)*
- *3 tablespoons grated Parmesan cheese*

1 Combine ricotta and mozzarella cheese and parsley.

2 Cut ends from zucchini and slice lengthwise into 5 mm (¼ in) strips. Arrange strips in a 20 cm (8 in) square microwave-safe dish. Cover with plastic wrap and cook on high 4 minutes. Rearrange strips during cooking. Drain well and cool slightly.

3 Place a layer of half the sliced zucchini on the bottom of the dish and spread ricotta mixture over. Cover with tomato slices and spread half tomato sauce over sliced tomatoes. Top with remaining zucchini strips. Pour over remaining sauce and sprinkle with Parmesan cheese.

4 Cook uncovered on medium 20 minutes. Let stand 5 minutes before serving.

Serve with Italian bread rolls.

Vegetable Lasagne

VEGETABLES WITH FRIED RICE

TIME: 9 MINUTES
SERVES 6

- *⅓ cup thinly sliced celery*
- *⅓ cup chopped green capsicum (pepper)*
- *⅓ cup chopped spring onions (shallots)*
- *1 small carrot, finely chopped*
- *250 g (8 oz) can sliced bamboo shoots, drained*
- *1 tablespoon vegetable oil*
- *1 teaspoon chopped parsley*
- *⅛ teaspoon salt*
- *⅛ teaspoon pepper*
- *1½ tablespoons soy sauce*
- *2 eggs, beaten*
- *2 cups cooked rice (⅔ cup raw)*

1 Combine vegetables, oil and seasonings in a bowl.

2 Preheat browning dish on high 3 minutes. Spoon in vegetable mixture and soy sauce, stir and cover. Cook on high 3 minutes or until crisp but still tender. Set aside.

3 Place eggs into a small bowl and cook on high 1 minute, stirring every 20 seconds.

4 Stir rice and eggs into vegetable mixture. Cook on high 2 minutes to heat through, stirring after 1 minute.

Serve with grilled fish, roast chicken or a Chinese meal.

PUMPKIN CHEESE RING

TIME: 19 MINUTES
SERVES 6 TO 8

> ½ cup chopped spring onions (shallots)
>
> 30 g (1 oz) butter
>
> 4 cups cooked, mashed pumpkin
>
> ½ teaspoon salt
>
> ¼ teaspoon cayenne pepper
>
> ¼ teaspoon ground nutmeg
>
> 1 cup (125 g/4 oz) freshly grated Parmesan cheese
>
> 4 eggs, beaten

1 Place spring onions and butter in a medium-sized bowl. Cover and cook on high 1 minute. Stir in remaining ingredients.

2 Pour into a greased 23 cm (9 in) microwave safe ring mould. Cook on high 18 minutes or until set. Let stand 8 minutes before turning out.

Serve with crisp bread rolls and a green salad.

BRAISED RED CABBAGE

TIME: 12 MINUTES
SERVES 6

> ½ red cabbage, thinly sliced
>
> 30 g (1 oz) butter
>
> 2 green apples, peeled, cored and sliced
>
> 1 small onion, chopped
>
> ½ teaspoon salt
>
> ¼ teaspoon pepper
>
> 2 cloves
>
> 1 bay leaf
>
> 2 tablespoons tarragon vinegar
>
> 1 cup (250 ml/8 fl oz) dry red wine
>
> 1 to 2 tablespoons brown sugar

1 Combine all ingredients in a microwave-safe casserole.

2 Cook covered on high 12 minutes, stirring every 4 minutes.

Serve with pork or sausages.

SPINACH BALLS

TIME: 12 TO 13 MINUTES
SERVES 6 TO 8

> 300 g (9½ oz) packet frozen spinach
>
> ¾ cup (90 g/3 oz) grated tasty cheese
>
> ¼ cup (30 g/1 oz) dry breadcrumbs
>
> 2 tablespoons Parmesan cheese
>
> 1 tablespoon finely chopped spring onions (shallots)
>
> ½ teaspoon salt
>
> ¼ teaspoon pepper
>
> 1 egg, beaten

1 Cook spinach in packet on high 5 minutes or until defrosted. Drain all excess liquid.

2 Combine chopped spinach with remaining ingredients and shape into balls 2 cm (¾ in) in diameter.

3 Place into a large shallow microwave-safe dish lined with paper towel and cook on high 2 minutes then on medium 5 to 6 minutes, until hot. Rearrange balls during cooking to ensure that all heat evenly.

Serve with grilled fish or roast chicken.

TOMATOES WITH SPINACH TOPPING

TIME: 10 MINUTES
SERVES 6

> 300 g (9½ oz) frozen, chopped spinach
>
> 3 large ripe tomatoes
>
> ⅛ teaspoon salt
>
> ⅛ teaspoon pepper
>
> ½ teaspoon sugar
>
> 1 tablespoon chopped fresh basil
>
> ½ cup (60 g/2 oz) grated cheese
>
> ¼ cup chopped onion

1 Cut corner off frozen spinach bag. Cook on high 5 to 6 minutes. Place spinach in a bowl and drain.

2 Cut the tomatoes in half using a decorative zig-zag cut, and sprinkle with salt, pepper, sugar and basil.

3 Combine half the cheese and all the onion with spinach. Spoon mixture into tomato halves and cook on high 4 minutes.

4 Top tomatoes with remaining cheese after cooking for 3 minutes.

Serve with fish, chicken or veal.

GAZPACHO

TIME: 1 MINUTE
SERVES 4 TO 6

> 250 g (8 oz) ripe tomatoes
>
> 60 g (2 oz) bread, crusts removed
>
> 2 tablespoons olive oil
>
> 2½ cups (600 ml/20 fl oz) chicken stock
>
> 1 clove garlic, peeled
>
> 1 tablespoon vinegar
>
> salt and pepper to taste
>
> 1 teaspoon sugar

ACCOMPANIMENTS

> 60 g (2 oz) ripe tomatoes, diced
>
> 60 g (2 oz) green capsicum (pepper), diced
>
> 60 g (2 oz) cucumber, peeled, deseeded and diced
>
> 1 cup croûtons

1 Remove core from tomatoes and place tomatoes in microwave oven. Cook on high 1 minute. Peel tomatoes and chop roughly.

2 Place tomatoes and bread into a food processor or blender. Add oil and 1 cup stock and purée.

3 Cut garlic clove in half and rub the inside of serving bowl. Pour in remaining stock and vinegar.

4 Blend in tomato purée, salt, pepper and sugar and refrigerate until chilled.

Serve chilled accompaniments with soup in separate bowls.

ARRANGING VEGETABLES FOR COOKING

Arrangement is the secret of microwave cooking many foods with different cooking times. Place larger, denser textured vegetables around the edge of the plate. Make a second ring with medium cooking time inside these and place quicker cooking, delicate vegetables in the centre. Arranged thus the vegetables will cook evenly and look attractive.

VEGETABLE PLATTER

TIME: 12 TO 14 MINUTES
SERVES 6

> 200 g (6 oz) cauliflower
>
> 200 g (6 oz) broccoli
>
> 2 medium-sized carrots
>
> 200 g (6 oz) small new potatoes
>
> 1 cup peas, beans or zucchini rings

1 Wash vegetables and cut into even-sized pieces. Prick potatoes with a skewer.

2 Arrange cauliflower, broccoli, carrots and potatoes around edge of plate. Place peas in centre. Add 2 tablespoons cold water and season lightly.

3 Cover with lid or a double thickness of plastic wrap. Cook on high 12 to 14 minutes.

Serve with butter or hollandaise sauce (see Veal with Avocado and Hollandaise Sauce, page 58). Serve as an accompaniment to a main course.

VEGETABLE STIR FRY

TIME: 7 MINUTES
SERVES 2

> 8 spring onions (shallots)
>
> 1 clove garlic, crushed
>
> 1 teaspoon chopped fresh ginger
>
> 1 tablespoon vegetable oil
>
> 1 carrot, sliced diagonally
>
> 2 stalks celery, sliced diagonally
>
> ½ red capsicum (pepper), sliced
>
> 12 green beans
>
> 12 snow peas
>
> 1 teaspoon cornflour
>
> 2 tablespoons soy sauce
>
> 1 tablespoon mirin or dry sherry
>
> 1 tablespoon rice or cider vinegar
>
> ½ cup (125 ml/4 fl oz) vegetable stock

1 Cut spring onions into 5 cm (2 in) lengths and halve lengthwise. Place in a microwave browner dish with garlic, ginger and oil. Cover and cook on high 1 minute.

2 Add carrot, celery, capsicum, beans and snow peas, cover and cook on high 4 minutes.

3 Blend cornflour with remaining ingredients, stir into vegetables. Cover and cook on high for 2 minutes.

Serve with rice.

Gazpacho

HOMEMADE TOMATO SAUCE

TIME: 21 MINUTES
SERVES 4 TO 6

15 g (½ oz) butter

15 g (½ oz) bacon pieces

1 small onion, chopped

1 small carrot, chopped

1 stalk celery, chopped

½ teaspoon dried basil

6 teaspoons plain (all purpose) flour

1 tablespoon tomato paste

375 ml (12 fl oz) vegetable stock

1 clove garlic, chopped

salt and pepper

1 Place butter in a casserole. Cook on high 45 seconds then add bacon pieces, onion, carrot, celery and basil. Cover and cook on high 5 minutes, stirring after 2 minutes.

2 Blend in flour and cook on high 1 minute. Add tomato paste, stock, garlic and seasonings and cook on high 4 to 5 minutes until boiling.

3 Reduce power to medium and cook 10 minutes. Purée sauce.

Serve with pasta, eggs, fish or meat and use in Vegetable Lasagne.

ZUCCHINI SPECIAL

TIME: 8 MINUTES
SERVES 4

500 g (1 lb) unpeeled zucchini, sliced

15 g (½ oz) butter

onion or garlic salt

1 teaspoon chopped fresh dill

1 large tomato, peeled, seeds removed, roughly chopped

1 Place all ingredients into a small casserole.

2 Cover and cook on high 8 minutes.

Serve with lamb, beef or chicken.

BOUQUET GARNI

10 x 5 cm (2 in) parsley stalks

3 large bay leaves

2 x 5 cm (2 in) pieces celery

Place parsley stalks and bay leaves into the hollow of one piece of celery. Place second piece of celery on top. Secure with string. Use to flavour soups, stocks and casseroles.

MINESTRONE

TIME: 26 MINUTES
SERVES 8

1 medium-sized onion, chopped

1 clove garlic, finely chopped

½ cup chopped celery

¼ cup diced green capsicum (pepper)

1 tablespoon olive oil

440 g (14 oz) can kidney beans

440 g (14 oz) can tomatoes

1 medium-sized zucchini, diced

¼ cup (60g/2 oz) white rice

3 cups (750 ml/24 fl oz) beef stock or consommé

¼ cup (60 ml/2 fl oz) red wine

1 tablespoon chopped parsley

pinch dried oregano

½ teaspoon sugar

¼ teaspoon white pepper

¼ cup (30 g/1 oz) grated Parmesan cheese

1 Place onion, garlic, celery, capsicum and oil in a 3 litre (96 fl oz) casserole dish. Cover and cook on high 6 minutes.

2 Add remaining ingredients except Parmesan cheese. Cover and cook on high 20 minutes, stirring 3 times during cooking.

Sprinkle with extra parsley and serve with Parmesan cheese.

BORSCHT

TIME: 22 MINUTES
SERVES 6 TO 8

250 g (8 oz) raw beetroot, grated

2 medium-sized carrots, thinly sliced

1 large onion, thinly sliced

1 medium-sized potato, cut in 1 cm (½ in) cubes

1½ cups shredded green cabbage

1 clove garlic, finely chopped

½ teaspoon salt

¼ teaspoon dried marjoram

⅛ teaspoon white pepper

1 large bay leaf

2½ cups (625 ml/20 fl oz) hot water

410 ml (13 fl oz) can beef consommé

sour cream

freshly cut dill

1 Place beetroot, carrots, onion, potato, cabbage, garlic, seasoning and ½ cup (125 ml/4 fl oz) water into a 3 litre (96 fl oz) casserole dish. Cover and cook on high 17 minutes or until vegetables are tender.

2 Add remaining water and beef consommé, cover and cook on high 15 minutes. Stir twice during cooking. Remove bay leaf.

3 Top individual servings with sour cream and dill to serve.

Prepare vegetables

Place vegetables in casserole

When vegetables are tender, add beef consommé

Borscht

Fresh Vegetable Cooking Chart

Artichokes, globe	Trim 2.5 cm (1 in) from top. Brush with fresh lemon juice. Cook 4 hearts in casserole, covered on high 10 to 14 minutes. Let stand 5 minutes.
Artichokes, Jerusalem	Can be roasted in their skins as potatoes, or washed, sliced and cooked in casserole dish. Add 2 tablespoons water, a squeeze of lemon juice and pinch of salt. Cover and cook on high 8 minutes per 500 g (1 lb).
Asparagus cuts	Place asparagus cuts into casserole dish. Add water if desired. Cover and cook on high 6 to 7 minutes per 500 g (1 lb).
Asparagus spears	Cut off tough end of each spear. Scrape off scales with potato peeler. Place spears in a single layer in casserole dish and add 2 tablespoons water. Cover and cook on high 5 minutes per 500 g (1 lb).
Beans, green, butter	Slice 500 g (1 lb) beans or cut into lengths. Place into casserole with 3 tablespoons cold water and 1 teaspoon vinegar. Cover and cook on high 12 minutes.
Beetroot	Wash 4 even-sized bulbs, trim tops leaving 2.5 cm (1 in) and root ends to prevent bleaching. Place into casserole with 2 tablespoons water. Cover and cook on high 16 to 20 minutes.
Broccoli	Trim and peel stalks, cut into individual florets. Place into casserole and add 3 tablespoons cold water. Cook on high 6 to 8 minutes per 500 g (1 lb).
Brussels sprouts	Trim wilted leaves, split stalks for even cooking. Place into casserole and add 2 tablespoons water. Cover and cook on high 6 to 8 minutes per 500 g (1 lb).
Cabbage, Chinese	Wash thoroughly, cut into 2.5 cm (1 in) lengths. Place into casserole and add 1 slice of shredded ginger, pinch of sugar, 2 tablespoons water and cook on high 6 to 8 minutes per 500 g (1 lb).
Cabbage, green	Shred or cut into serving wedges. Place into casserole and add 2 tablespoons water. Cover and cook on high 8 minutes per 500 g (1 lb).
Cabbage, red	Shred cabbage, place into casserole and add 2 teaspoons lemon juice, pinch of sugar, 2 tablespoons water. Cover and cook on high 8 to 12 minutes per 500 g (1 lb).
Capsicums (peppers)	Thinly slice and place in casserole dish with 1 tablespoon oil, garlic and seasonings. Cover and cook on high 5 minutes per 500 g (1 lb).
Carrots	Wash, peel, cut into even-sized pieces and place into casserole. Add 2 tablespoons water, cover and cook on high 8 minutes per 500 g (1 lb).
Cauliflower	Cut into serving pieces, wash. Place into casserole, add 2 tablespoons water, cover and cook on high 7 to 8 minutes per 500 g (1 lb).
Celery	Cut celery into even-sized pieces. Place into casserole and add 2 tablespoons butter or water, cover, cook on high 7 minutes per 500 g (1 lb).
Corn kernels	Place 500 g (1 lb) corn into casserole and add 2 tablespoons water. Cover and cook on high 8 minutes.
Corn-on-the-cob	Corn can be cooked in the husk or peeled and wrapped in clear plastic wrap. Place four cobs in microwave oven, spaced evenly. Cook on high 12 to 16 minutes, turn over half way through cooking.
Eggplant	Cut 750 g (1½ lb) eggplant into 2 cm (¾ in) cubes, place into casserole and add 2 tablespoons butter or water. Cover and cook on high 8 to 10 minutes. Season before serving.
Kohlrabi	Trim off root and stem, cut into slices or wedges. Place into casserole and add 2 tablespoons water, pinch of salt and cover. Cook on high 10 to 12 minutes per 1 kg (2 lb).

Leeks	Trim and peel 750 g (1 ½ lb). Split halfway through, place into casserole dish, add 2 tablespoons water, cover. Cook on high 6 minutes until tender.
Marrow	Peel, cut into serving pieces. Place into casserole, add 2 tablespoons butter, cover and cook on high 7 minutes per 500 g (1 lb).
Mushrooms, sliced	Place into casserole with 2 tablespoons butter. Cover and cook on high 4 minutes per 500 g (1 lb).
Mushrooms, whole	Trim stalks, place into casserole with 2 tablespoons butter. Cover and cook on high 4 to 5 minutes per 500 g (1 lb).
Okra, sliced	Cut into 1 cm (½ in) lengths. Place into casserole with 2 tablespoons water, pinch of salt. Cover and cook on high 7 to 8 minutes per 500 g (1 lb).
Okra, whole	Trim stalk from pods. Place into casserole and add 2 tablespoons water, pinch of salt, cover and cook on high 8 minutes per 500 g (1 lb).
Onions, sliced	Peel and slice or cut into wedges. Place into casserole with 2 tablespoons water or butter. Cook on high 8 minutes per 500 g (1 lb). Stir during cooking.
Onions, whole	Peel onions, place whole in casserole. Add 2 tablespoons butter or water and cook covered on high 8 minutes per 500 g (1 lb). Turn over during cooking.
Parsnips	Peel and cut into even-sized pieces. Place into casserole, add 2 tablespoons water. Cover and cook on high 7 to 8 minutes per 500 g (1 lb). Stir once.
Peas, green	Place 2 cups shelled peas into casserole dish and add 2 tablespoons water, pinch of sugar, sprig of mint. Cover and cook on high, for 6 to 7 minutes.
Peas, snow	Remove string from pods. Place into casserole, add 2 tablespoons water. Cover and cook on high 4 to 5 minutes per 250 g (8 oz).
Potatoes, whole	Prick 4 even-sized potatoes with skewer. Place evenly apart in oven. Cook on high 12 minutes, in jacket turn over during cooking.
Potatoes, pieces	Peel potatoes, cut into even-sized pieces. Place into casserole. Add 2 tablespoons water, pinch of salt. Cover and cook on high 8 to 12 minutes per 750 g (1 ½ lb). Rearrange during cooking.
Pumpkin	Peel, cut into serving pieces and place into casserole. Cover and cook on high 12 minutes per 1 kg (2 lb).
Silverbeet	Cook as for English spinach. Toss with melted butter and ground nutmeg.
Spinach, English	Wash and shred, cook covered in casserole on high 5 to 6 minutes per 500 g (1 lb). Cook in moisture that clings to leaves.
Squash	Cut baby squash into quarters. Place into casserole. Add 2 tablespoons butter or water. Cover and cook on high 6 to 7 minutes per 500 g (1 lb).
Sweet potato and yams	Wash potatoes, prick with skewer, cut into serving pieces and place in oven, evenly apart. Cook on high 11 to 13 minutes per 750g (1 ½ lb).
Tomatoes, sliced or wedges	Arrange in casserole. Season and cover. Cook on high 3 minutes per 500 g (1 lb).
Tomatoes, whole	To cook 4 whole or stuffed tomatoes. Cover and cook on high 2 to 4 minutes.
Turnips	Peel and slice. Place into casserole and add 2 tablespoons water. Cover and cook on high 10 to 11 minutes per 750 g (1 ½ lb).
Zucchini	Wash, cut into 1 cm (½ in) sticks, place into casserole, add 2 tablespoons butter. Cover and cook on high 6 to 7 minutes per 500 g (1 lb).

Seafood Specials

Seafood cooked in a microwave oven retains its shape and natural fresh flavour. It is an important source of easy-to-digest protein, minerals and vitamins. The seafood recipes that follow include shellfish, white fish, fillets and steaks, whole fish, stuffed fish and even smoked fish. They will inspire you to prepare and serve some delicious fish dishes.

DON'T OVERCOOK THESE FOODS

When using ingredients such as asparagus, mushrooms, cheese, strawberries or shellfish it is always best to add them to the mixture toward the end of the microwaving process so that these fairly sensitive foods are not overcooked.

PREPARING SCALLOPS AND OPENING MOLLUSC SHELLS

To prepare scallops, remove the beard, which is brownish coloured and usually found near the coral. The intestinal track should also be removed. Split large scallops in half before cooking. Fresh scallops, clams and oysters in the shell may be opened in the microwave oven. First clean the shells and soak in cold water for 10 minutes. Place 6 shells at a time around edge of pie plate, cover with lid or plastic wrap and cook on high 45 seconds or until shells have just opened. Continue to heat any unopened shells, checking every 15 seconds. Insert knife between shells to open.

PRAWN CREOLE

TIME: 13 MINUTES
SERVES 4 TO 6

500 g (1 lb) can tomato pieces

1 medium-sized onion, diced in 1 cm (½ in) pieces

1 green capsicum (pepper), diced in 1 cm (½ in) pieces

½ teaspoon salt

½ teaspoon white pepper

½ teaspoon chilli powder

1 bay leaf

500 g (1 lb) green prawns, shelled and deveined

1 Combine all ingredients except prawns in a 1.5 litre (48 fl oz) casserole dish. Cover and cook on high 9 minutes, stirring once.

2 Stir in prawns, cover and cook on medium-high 4 to 5 minutes, stirring twice during cooking.

3 Avoid overcooking as this toughens prawns. Remove bay leaf before serving.

Serve with Lemon Rice (page 70).

WHOLE BABY CRAYFISH WITH LEMON BUTTER SAUCE

TIME: 15 MINUTES
SERVES 2

2 medium-sized crayfish (lobsters), halved

salt and pepper to taste

½ teaspoon chopped fresh thyme

½ teaspoon chopped fresh oregano

30 g (1 oz) butter, melted

1 lemon, sliced

LEMON BUTTER

grated rind of 1 lemon

90 g (3 oz) butter, melted

salt and pepper to taste

1 Place crayfish halves in a shallow casserole dish. Season with salt, pepper, thyme, oregano and butter. Top with lemon slices. Cover and cook on medium 15 minutes. Allow to stand covered.

2 Remove tail meat from shell, slice neatly and return to tail shells.

3 To make lemon butter, blend lemon rind, melted butter, salt and pepper till smooth.

Serve crayfish halves with lemon slices and lemon butter dotted on each tail, accompanied with Lemon Rice (page 70).

CRAB MOUSSE

TIME: 1 MINUTE
SERVES 8 TO 10

1 tablespoon gelatine

2 tablespoons cold water

400 g (13 oz) crabmeat, flaked

2 teaspoons fresh lemon juice

2 tablespoons white wine

⅔ cup (160 ml/5 fl oz) mayonnaise

⅔ cup (160 ml/5 fl oz) sour cream

¼ teaspoon cayenne pepper

pepper

1 packet toast squares

1 Place gelatine and water in cup or small bowl and cook on high 1 minute. Stir and allow to cool slightly.

2 Combine crabmeat, lemon juice, wine, mayonnaise, sour cream and peppers. Gradually add gelatine mixture and blend.

3 Spoon mixture into a prepared 4 cup (1 litre/32 fl oz) mould. Chill for 2 to 3 hours. When firm, unmould.

Serve as an entrée with a salad garnish or as a party savoury accompanied with toast squares.

FISH WITH ORANGE CORIANDER SAUCE

TIME: 9 MINUTES
SERVES 4

60 g (2 oz) butter

1 tablespoon cornflour

juice of 1 large orange

juice of 1 lemon

*2 tablespoons chopped fresh
coriander*

1 tablespoon chopped fresh chives

1 stalk lemon grass, thinly sliced

¼ teaspoon salt

¼ teaspoon white pepper

*4 portions ling or perch fillet;
approximately 750 g (1½ lb),
skinned*

*4 tablespoons toasted slivered
almonds*

Fish with Orange Coriander Sauce

1 Place butter in a microwave browning casserole, cover and cook on high 1 minute.

2 Blend cornflour with orange and lemon juices. Stir into butter with herbs, lemon grass, salt and pepper.

3 Dip fish fillets into orange mixture, then arrange skinned side down with thickest parts near edge of dish. Cover and cook on high 4 minutes.

4 Baste fish with sauce, sprinkle with almonds and cook, covered, on medium 4 minutes or until cooked. The fish will flake easily. Stir sauce well before serving.

Serve with Baby Buttered Potatoes (page 16) and a green vegetable.

ROLLMOPS

TIME: 5 MINUTES
SERVES 10 TO 12

*2 salt herrings, cleaned and
filleted*

*4 cups (1 litre/32 fl oz) cold
water*

1 onion, thinly sliced

1 cup (250 ml/8 fl oz) water

1 tablespoon peppercorns

1 bay leaf

1 tablespoon capers

*1 tablespoon dried dill
(or 3 tablespoons fresh)*

parsley sprigs to garnish

1 Place herring fillets into cold water. Allow to soak 3 hours. Drain. Place herring and onion rings in layers in a shallow dish.

2 Combine 1 cup water, peppercorns, bay leaf, capers and dill. Pour over herrings. Cover and cook on medium 5 minutes.

3 Allow to chill overnight in refrigerator. Drain off liquid. Remove bay leaf and peppercorns.

Serve with a potato and a green salad.

JEWFISH CUTLETS WITH CREAMY SAUCE

TIME: 19½ MINUTES
SERVES 6

> 6 medium jewfish cutlets
> 15 g (½ oz) butter
> 125 g (4 oz) mushrooms, sliced
> 60 g (2 oz) scallops, poached
> 6 spring onions (shallots), finely chopped
> 2 tablespoons fresh lemon juice
> ⅔ cup (150 ml/5 fl oz) cream
> 1 tablespoon cornflour
> 1 teaspoon chopped fresh dill
> pine nuts, to garnish

1 Arrange jewfish cutlets in a shallow microwave-safe dish in a single layer. Cover and cook on medium 10 to 15 minutes.

2 Melt butter in a 1 litre (32 fl oz) casserole on high 30 seconds. Add mushrooms, scallops, spring onions and lemon juice. Cover and cook on medium 2 minutes, stirring once.

3 Blend together cream, cornflour and dill. Add to mushroom mixture and stir. Cook on medium-high 2 minutes. Stir.

4 Arrange jewfish cutlets on a serving platter and pour over creamy sauce. Garnish with pine nuts.

Serve with Baby Buttered Potatoes (page 16) and salad.

CRAB STUFFED FLOUNDER FILLETS

TIME: 22 MINUTES
SERVES 4

> 8 thin, evenly sized, flounder fillets
> 15 g (½ oz) butter
> ½ cup chopped onion
> ½ cup chopped red capsicum (pepper)
> 300 g (10 oz) flaked crabmeat
> 4 tablespoons fresh breadcrumbs
> 1 teaspoon parsley
> ½ teaspoon salt
> ½ teaspoon lemon pepper
> ¾ cup (185 ml/6 fl oz) tomato juice
> ½ teaspoon chopped basil
> 1 teaspoon lemon juice
> 4 lemon slices

1 Wash, dry and trim flounder fillets.

2 Combine butter, onion and capsicum in a bowl and cook on high 4 minutes, stirring once during cooking.

3 Stir in crabmeat, breadcrumbs, parsley, salt and lemon pepper.

4 Arrange 4 flounder fillets in a large, shallow dish, cover each evenly with stuffing mixture then place a second fillet on top.

5 Combine tomato juice, basil and lemon juice in a bowl and cook on high 2 minutes. Spoon sauce over fillets and top with lemon slices. Cook on medium 16 minutes or until fish flakes easily.

Serve with rice or Baby Buttered Potatoes (page 16) and a green vegetable.

Combine butter, onion and capsicum

Stir in crabmeat and breadcrumbs

Cover each fillet with stuffing

Layer salmon and brie on pastry case

Combine remaining filling ingredients

Spoon egg mixture into crust

BRIE AND SMOKED SALMON FLAN

TIME: 23 MINUTES
SERVES 6

PASTRY

> 1½ cups (185 g/6 oz) plain (all purpose) flour
>
> salt to taste
>
> 2 teaspoons ground black pepper
>
> 2 teaspoons mixed herbs
>
> 30 g (1 oz) butter
>
> 15 g (½ oz) lard
>
> cold water

FILLING

> 125 g (4 oz) smoked salmon, sliced
>
> 250 g (8 oz) Brie cheese, sliced
>
> 1¼ cups (300 ml/10 fl oz) cream
>
> 3 eggs, beaten
>
> 2 tablespoons chopped fresh herbs
>
> 1 teaspoon pepper
>
> 4 spring onions (shallots), chopped
>
> paprika

1 Combine flour, salt, pepper and mixed herbs. Rub in butter and lard. Mix through enough water to form a soft dough, like a scone dough.

2 Knead dough lightly on a floured board, roll out and line individual ceramic tartlet dishes or a 23 cm (9 in) pie plate. Trim edges and prick base of dough with fork. Cook pastry on high 6 to 8 minutes. Allow to cool slightly before filling.

3 Layer salmon then cheese on pastry base. Combine remaining filling ingredients, except paprika, and pour into crust. Sprinkle top lightly with paprika and cook on medium 10 to 15 minutes.

Serve as an entrée or a light meal with salad.

STUFFED TROUT

TIME: 7 MINUTES
SERVES 2

> 2 whole trout, 250 g (8 oz) each
>
> 3 spring onions (shallots), finely chopped
>
> 30 g (1 oz) butter
>
> 2 tablespoons coarsely chopped cashews
>
> 60 g (2 oz) small shelled prawns
>
> 1 cup chopped, blanched broccoli
>
> ¼ teaspoon salt
>
> ¼ teaspoon lemon pepper
>
> 1 teaspoon fresh lemon juice, strained

1 Wash and dry trout, remove any remaining scales. Place spring onions and butter in a small bowl. Cook on high 1 minute.

2 Add cashews, prawns, broccoli, salt and pepper.

3 Place trout in a baking dish in a single layer with the thickest part of the fish to the outside of the dish. Spoon prepared mixture into cavity of each fish. Arrange remaining mixture around trout and sprinkle with lemon juice.

4 Cover and cook on high 6 minutes or until fish flakes.

Serve with rice and salad.

WARMING MILK

Warm milk before blending into roux-based sauces. This avoids lumps and forms the sauce quickly. The sauce should always boil before serving.

WHOLE SILVER BREAM WITH CHILLI GINGER SAUCE

TIME: 20 MINUTES
SERVES 4

SAUCE

- 3 tablespoons oil
- 4 red chillies, deseeded and finely chopped
- 3 slices ginger, finely chopped
- 2 cloves garlic, finely chopped
- 3 tablespoons finely chopped onion
- 1½ tablespoons dry sherry
- 4 tablespoons tomato sauce
- 1 tablespoon sugar
- 3 tablespoons white vinegar
- 2 spring onions (shallots), shredded, to garnish

FISH

- 1 whole silver bream or snapper, approximately 1 kg (2 lb)
- 2 tablespoons fresh lemon juice
- ½ teaspoon salt

1 Place oil into a bowl, add chillies, ginger, garlic and onion. Cover and cook on high 4 minutes, stirring after 2 minutes. Add sherry, tomato sauce, sugar and vinegar. Cook on medium 6 minutes, stirring every 2 minutes. Sauce can be made in advance and stored in refrigerator. Reheat just before serving.

2 Trim fins and tail of fish. Remove eyes using a melon baller or prick eyes to prevent them from bursting. Cut the thickest section of the fish three times on each side to enable the fish to cook evenly.

3 Place fish onto a serving plate.

Whole Silver Bream with Chilli Ginger Sauce

Rub inside of fish with salt. Squeeze lemon juice over fish. Cover with plastic wrap. Cook on medium 8 to 10 minutes. Test with fork. The flesh should flake easily if cooked.

4 Drain any juice from platter. Pour chilli ginger sauce over fish and top with shredded spring onions.

Serve hot, accompanied with rice and crisp green salad.

QUICK FISH STOCK

TIME: 11 MINUTES
MAKES 3 CUPS
(750 ML/24 FL OZ)

100 g (3 oz) white fish fillets
1 tablespoon chopped onion
1 bay leaf
1 teaspoon fresh lemon juice
4 parsley stalks
3 peppercorns
2 cups (500 ml/16 fl oz) water

1 Place all ingredients in a 2 litre (64 fl oz) casserole. Cover and cook on high 6 minutes. Stir. Cook on medium 5 minutes, then strain.

2 Correct seasonings before using.

FISH STOCK

Do not add fish skins to the stock as they will make it too dark.

If stock is bitter, it has boiled for too long or the bones were not washed properly.

If too liquid or cloudy, you have probably added too much water or covered the stock during cooking. For the water to draw out the flavours from the bones it must cover them, but beware of adding too much water.

If stock is cloudy you did not skim often enough. Skimming when scum first begins to gather on top of the stock and before the stock reaches simmering point is more important than at any other stage.

CURRIED SMOKED COD SUPREME

TIME: 25 MINUTES
SERVES 6

500 g (1 lb) smoked cod
15 g (½ oz) butter
250 g (8 oz) onions, thinly sliced
2 teaspoons curry powder
30 g (1 oz) butter
2 tablespoons plain (all purpose) flour
2 cups (500 ml/16 fl oz) milk
½ teaspoon salt
¼ teaspoon pepper
¼ cup (60 ml/2 fl oz) white wine
2 tablespoons mayonnaise
½ cup (60 g/2 oz) grated cheese
½ teaspoon paprika

1 Place cod fillets into a plastic bag or baking dish. Cook on high 5 minutes. Remove any bones and skin, flake fish with a fork and set aside.

2 Melt 15 g butter in a bowl on high 1 minute. Add onions, and cook 4 to 5 minutes, covered, on high. Stir twice during cooking. Add curry powder, cook 1 minute on high and set aside.

3 Melt 30 g butter in jug on high 1 minute. Stir in flour and cook 2 minutes on high. Stir in milk and cook on high 5 to 6 minutes until boiling, stirring twice during cooking. Add salt, pepper, wine and mayonnaise.

4 Place a layer of half the sauce in a 20 x 20 cm (8 x 8 in) casserole dish. Cover with onions and the flaked cod. Cover evenly with remaining sauce. Sprinkle with grated cheese and paprika and cook on medium 6 minutes. Let stand 3 minutes before serving.

Serve accompanied with rice and salad.

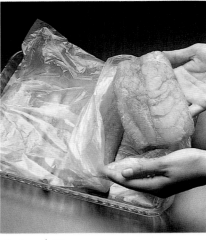

Cook cod fillets in plastic bag

Add curry powder to cooked onions

Cover onions and flaked cod with sauce

Curried Smoked Cod Supreme

Speedy Creations with Chicken

*C*hicken, particularly pieces, cook very quickly in the microwave oven. A large, shallow microwave browning casserole is a good investment for cooking chicken successfully. You will be delighted with the tasty, tender results and you will have more time to relax and enjoy them.

TASTY THAI CHICKEN

TIME: 8 MINUTES
SERVES 4

1 teaspoon chopped fresh ginger

2 stalks lemon grass, thinly sliced

2 spring onions (shallots), thinly sliced

1 tablespoon green curry paste

1 clove garlic, crushed

400 ml (13 fl oz) can coconut milk

500 g (1 lb) chicken breast fillets, cut in 1 x 5 cm (½ x 2 in) strips

½ cup chopped fresh coriander leaves

juice of 1 lime

1 teaspoon fish sauce or salt to taste

1 Place ginger, lemon grass, spring onions, green curry paste, garlic and coconut milk in a microwave browning casserole. Cover and cook on high 3 minutes.

2 Stir well, add chicken and stir until every piece is coated. Cover and cook on high 5 minutes or until tender.

3 Stir in coriander leaves, lime juice and fish sauce before serving.

Serve with rice.

Recipes on previous pages: Fijian Chicken (page 45), Mexican Salsa Chicken (page 46)

COQ AU VIN

TIME: 30 MINUTES
SERVES 6

1.5 kg (3 lb) chicken thighs

4 slices bacon, diced into 2 cm (¾ in) pieces

⅓ cup (45 g/1½ oz) plain (all purpose) flour

½ cup (125 ml/4 fl oz) red wine

½ cup (125 ml/4 fl oz) chicken stock

2 tablespoons brandy

2 teaspoon chopped parsley

1 teaspoon salt

1 clove garlic, finely chopped

1 bay leaf

1 teaspoon chopped fresh thyme

¼ teaspoon pepper

250 g (8 oz) mushrooms, sliced

1 large onion, sliced

1 Wash and dry chicken well. Place bacon in a 3 litre (96 fl oz) casserole dish. Cover and cook on high 4 minutes. Drain, leaving 1 tablespoon bacon fat in casserole. Blend in flour. Stir in liquids and seasonings.

2 Add mushrooms, onion and chicken. Cover and cook on high 15 minutes. Stir and rearrange chicken. Cook on medium 11 minutes or until chicken is tender. Let stand, covered, 5 minutes before serving.

Serve with Baby Buttered Potatoes (page 16) and Honey Glazed Carrots (page 14).

ASIAN CHICKEN WITH APRICOTS

TIME: 14 MINUTES
SERVES 4

4 chicken breast fillets

8 fresh asparagus spears

freshly ground pepper

30 g (1 oz) butter

2 cloves garlic, crushed

1 tablespoon curry paste or powder

425 g (14 oz) can apricots in light syrup

2 tablespoons mango chutney

1 teaspoon chopped fresh ginger (or ¼ teaspoon ground)

2 tablespoons teriyaki sauce

3 teaspoons cornflour

1 Cut the membranes attaching the tenderloin fillets to the chicken breasts and fold to one side, making the breast fillets thinner and wider. Place between clear plastic and beat until 1 cm (½ in) thick.

2 Cut asparagus into lengths a little longer than width of chicken breasts and place across centre. Roll chicken up from top to bottom of breasts and secure with toothpicks. Sprinkle with pepper.

3 Place butter, garlic and curry in a microwave browning dish, cover and cook on high 1 minute.

Whole Chicken Breasts Florentine Style

4 Place chicken around edge of dish, cover and cook on high 1 minute. Drain apricots and reserve ½ cup (125 ml/4 fl oz) syrup. Mix syrup with chutney, ginger and teriyaki sauce and pour over chicken. Cover and cook on medium 5 minutes.

5 Add apricots, cover and cook on medium a further 5 minutes. Blend cornflour with 2 tablespoons apricot syrup, stir in and cook covered on medium 2 minutes.

Serve with rice and green beans or snow peas.

WHOLE CHICKEN BREASTS FLORENTINE STYLE

TIME: 9 MINUTES
SERVES 4

> ¼ cup grated carrot
>
> ¼ cup pine nuts
>
> 250 g (8 oz) frozen spinach, thawed, drained and chopped
>
> 2 cloves garlic, crushed
>
> salt and pepper to taste
>
> 2 tablespoons chopped parsley
>
> 4 chicken breast fillets
>
> 1 egg, beaten
>
> 1 tablespoon water
>
> pinch ground nutmeg
>
> 1 cup (125 g/4 oz) seasoned dry breadcrumbs
>
> 1 tablespoon oil

1 Combine carrot, pine nuts, spinach, garlic, salt, pepper and parsley. Fill centre of chicken breasts with small portion of spinach mixture. Fold over and secure with wooden skewer or tie with string.

2 Blend egg and water. Combine nutmeg and breadcrumbs. Dip chicken breasts in egg mix and coat with breadcrumb mixture.

3 Place on an oiled microwave roasting (grilling) rack and cook on high 9 minutes, turning once during the cooking.

Serve hot accompanied with new potatoes and grilled tomatoes.

CHICKEN BREASTS IN BACON

TIME: 7 MINUTES
SERVES 2

2 chicken breast fillets

2 rashers bacon

1 teaspoon finely chopped fresh ginger

15 g (½ oz) butter

2 tablespoons fresh lemon juice

freshly ground black pepper

1 Remove skin from chicken breasts and discard, remove any fat and tissues with kitchen scissors. Open out each fillet carefully from each chicken breast without detaching it, to form chicken breast portions into an even thickness.

2 Remove rind and bones from bacon rashers. Place bacon rashers obliquely on a chopping board, place a chicken breast horizontally on top of each rasher, sprinkle with ginger. Wrap bacon securely around each fillet.

3 Place a microwave browning dish in oven on high for 2 minutes. Remove dish with oven gloves, add butter and swirl around to cover bottom of dish, then quickly place bacon wrapped chicken breasts in and leave until butter stops sizzling.

4 Turn bacon wrapped chicken over carefully, pour lemon juice over and sprinkle with freshly ground black pepper. Cover dish and cook on high 5 minutes.

Serve hot, accompanied with boiled brown rice tossed with butter and chopped chives and green peas or snow peas.

CHICKEN ROULADE WITH ALMOND AND BROCCOLI STUFFING

TIME: 12 MINUTES
SERVES 4

4 large chicken breast fillets, skin removed

4 slices cheddar cheese

300 g (10 oz) frozen broccoli, defrosted and chopped

60 g (2 oz) almonds or cashews, chopped

1 cup (250 ml/8 fl oz) milk

1 tablespoon plain (all purpose) flour

1 tablespoon white wine

2 teaspoons chopped parsley

¼ teaspoon salt

¼ teaspoon pepper

1 tablespoon grated cheese

1 Pound chicken fillets to flatten. Place a piece of cheese onto each fillet and divide broccoli and almonds between the four chicken fillets. Roll up fillets around broccoli and secure with cocktail sticks.

2 Place rolls seam side down in 20 cm (8 in) square baking dish. Cover with white kitchen paper towel and cook on high 8 minutes, turning twice during cooking. Drain and set aside.

3 Blend milk, flour, wine, parsley, salt and pepper in a jug. Cook on high 2 to 3 minutes until thickened, stirring twice during cooking. Blend in grated cheese.

4 Pour sauce over roulade and cook on high 1 minute to reheat.

Serve accompanied with rice and a green vegetable.

CHICKEN DIJONNAISE

TIME: 28 MINUTES
SERVES 4

1 onion, chopped

1 tablespoon mustard seeds

30 g (1 oz) butter

500 g (1 lb) chicken thighs

2 tablespoons Dijon mustard

½ cup (125 ml/4 fl oz) dry white wine

½ cup (125 ml/4 fl oz) chicken stock

1 tablespoon capers

2 tablespoons chopped fresh chives

2 teaspoons cornflour

½ cup (125 ml/4 fl oz) light sour cream

1 Place onion, mustard seeds and butter in a microwave browning casserole, cover and cook on high 2 minutes. Add chicken and arrange thickest parts near edge of dish.

2 Mix remaining ingredients, except cornflour and sour cream, and pour over chicken. Cover and cook on high 6 minutes then on medium 10 minutes.

3 Blend cornflour with cream, stir into chicken and cook on medium a further 10 minutes.

Serve with new potatoes or rice and a green vegetable.

CHICKEN IN SPICY SAUCE

TIME: 30 MINUTES
SERVES 8

> 2 x 1.5 kg (3 lb) roasting
>   chickens
> 1 tablespoon oil
> 1 teaspoon chilli sauce
> 1 tablespoon paprika
> 1 teaspoon celery salt
> freshly ground black pepper

1 Cut chickens into quarters. Combine oil and chilli sauce and brush onto chicken quarters. Place chicken portions in a shallow microwave browning casserole.

2 Combine paprika, celery salt and pepper. Sprinkle over chicken.

Cover and cook on medium-high 20 minutes. Rearrange chicken and cook uncovered a further 10 minutes. Stand 5 minutes. Alternatively, barbecue 10 minutes to complete cooking.

Serve with Spicy Rice with Peas (page 70) and Gado Gado Salad (page 11).

TESTING IF A WHOLE CHICKEN IS COOKED

Pierce thigh with a cocktail stick. If liquid runs clear the chicken is cooked. Should the natural juice have a slight pink colour — this may occur if chicken was frozen — the chicken requires longer cooking.

CRAB STUFFED CHICKEN

TIME: 20 TO 30 MINUTES
SERVES 4 TO 6

> 1.5 kg (3 lb) whole chicken

STUFFING

> 150 g (5 oz) crabmeat
> ½ cup chopped green capsicum
>   (pepper)
> 1 tomato, chopped
> 1 teaspoon fresh lemon juice
> ¼ teaspoon pepper
> 2 slices bread cut in 1 cm (½ in)
>   cubes

GLAZE

> 2 teaspoons soy sauce
> 1 tablespoon white wine
> 2½ tablespoons water
> 1 teaspoon cornflour
> ⅛ teaspoon garlic salt

1 Weigh chicken and allow 8 to 9 minutes cooking time on high per 500 g (1 lb). Combine remaining stuffing ingredients in bowl. Place inside cavity of chicken and truss with white kitchen string.

2 To make glaze, blend all glaze ingredients together in a bowl and cook on high 2 minutes, stirring after 1 minute.

3 Place chicken on a roasting (grilling) rack, breast side down. Brush with prepared glaze. Cook on high for half required time. Turn chicken breast side up and baste with remaining glaze. Cook on high for remainder of time.

Serve with rice and Vegetable Stir Fry (page 21).

Combine stuffing ingredients

Place stuffing in chicken

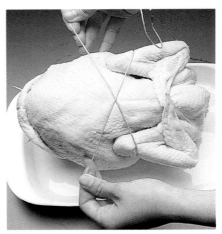
Truss chicken with kitchen string

CHICKEN AND AVOCADO SALAD

TIME: 10 MINUTES
SERVES 8

8 chicken breast fillets

1 tablespoon oil

1 teaspoon paprika

1 tablespoon chopped parsley

1 teaspoon chopped fresh oregano

410 g (13 oz) fresh or canned seedless grapes

2 avocados

6 spring onions (shallots), chopped

8 radishes, sliced

¼ cup (60 ml/2 fl oz) sour cream

dash tabasco sauce

1 Place chicken fillets in a shallow dish with thickest parts near edge. Coat with oil and sprinkle with paprika, parsley and oregano.

2 Cover with lid or plastic wrap and cook on medium high 10 minutes. Stand 5 minutes then cut chicken into strips.

3 Drain grapes and add to chicken pieces. Peel and roughly chop avocado. Add avocado, spring onions and radishes to chicken mix. Toss salad together.

4 Blend together sour cream and tabasco sauce. Serve sauce on chicken and avocado salad or separately.

Serve with a pasta or rice salad and a green salad, or as part of a buffet salad menu.

CHICKEN AND EGGPLANT CACCIATORE

TIME: 20 MINUTES
SERVES 4

500 g (1 lb) boneless chicken thighs

1 cup eggplant (aubergine), cut in 1 cm (½ in) cubes

4 tablespoons French dressing

500 ml (16 fl oz) jar cacciatore or napolitana sauce

1 Remove any skin from chicken and cut thighs in half.

2 Mix eggplant with French dressing. Place chicken, eggplant and dressing in a microwave-safe casserole with the thickest part of the chicken at the edge of the dish. Cover and cook on high 5 minutes.

3 Add sauce, stir well then cover and cook on medium 15 minutes, stirring after 7 minutes.

Serve with rice or pasta noodles and a green vegetable.

Chicken and Avocado Salad

FIJIAN CHICKEN

TIME: 11 MINUTES
SERVES 4

    15 g (½ oz) butter

    2 tablespoons sliced spring onions (shallots)

    1 tablespoon chopped fresh ginger

    4 cloves garlic, crushed

    4 chicken breast fillets

    ½ cup (125 ml/4 fl oz) coconut milk

    2 tablespoons peanut butter

    1 large lime

    1½ cups pawpaw balls

1 Place butter, spring onions, ginger and garlic in a microwave browning casserole, cover and cook on high 2 minutes.

2 Place chicken breasts in corners of casserole, turn over until well coated with butter mixture.

3 Add coconut milk and peanut butter. Cover and cook on high for 8 minutes, stirring after 5 minutes.

4 Peel lime rind thinly and cut into julienne strips. Squeeze lime. Add lime julienne, juice and pawpaw to chicken, stir well and cook covered on high 1 minute.

Serve with rice and a green vegetable or salad.

Fijian Chicken

CUTTING VEGETABLES

When preparing vegetables for casseroles bear in mind that smaller, evenly cut pieces microwave faster than large, irregularly cut vegetables.

ORANGE PECAN DRUMSTICKS

TIME: 23 MINUTES
SERVES 4 TO 6

1.5 to 2 kg (3 to 4 lb) chicken drumsticks, skin removed

180 ml (6 fl oz) concentrated orange juice

½ cup (125 ml/4 fl oz) water

1 chicken stock cube, crumbled

½ teaspoon salt

¼ cup (60 ml/2 fl oz) water

2 tablespoons cornflour or arrowroot

½ cup finely chopped spring onions (shallots)

½ cup pecan nuts

1 Place drumsticks in a microwave browning dish with the meaty ends arranged around the edge. Combine orange juice, ½ cup water, stock cube and salt in jug. Pour sauce over chicken, cover and cook on high 20 minutes until tender.

2 Remove drumsticks to a serving platter.

3 Combine ¼ cup water with cornflour or arrowroot in a medium-sized bowl. Blend arrowroot into sauce. Add spring onions and pecan nuts. Cook on high 2 to 3 minutes, stirring after 1 minute. Pour sauce over drumsticks.

Serve with rice and a green vegetable.

LOW FAT CHICKEN

Remove skin from chicken drumsticks to reduce fat, cholesterol and kilojoules. Skin is easily removed from chicken pieces. Simply ease fingertips under skin and pull.

TANGY BARBECUE DRUMSTICKS

TIME: 25 MINUTES
SERVES 4

8 large chicken drumsticks

juice and rind of 1 orange

1 tablespoon honey

½ teaspoon chilli sauce

1 tablespoon barbecue sauce

freshly ground black pepper

1 tablespoon oil

1 teaspoon dried thyme

1 Trim chicken drumsticks neatly. Remove skin if desired.

2 Combine orange juice and rind, honey, chilli sauce, barbecue sauce, pepper, oil and thyme in a glass jug. Cook on high 1 minute.

3 Coat drumsticks with baste. Place in a shallow microwave browning dish with thick end near the edge of dish. Cook on high 4 minutes, then medium-high 10 minutes, turn and cook a further 10 minutes or until juice runs clear.

Serve with rice and a green salad.

TO CHANGE YIELD

To increase or decrease the yield of a microwave recipe, follow these hints: Decreasing yield by half — use only half the specified quantity of ingredients and reduce cooking time by one-third. Doubling yield — double quantity of solid ingredients, increase liquids by one and two-thirds to one and three-quarters and increase cooking time by about half to two-thirds.

MEXICAN SALSA CHICKEN

TIME: 27 MINUTES
SERVES 4

8 chicken wings

1 onion, chopped

2 red chillies, seeded and sliced

2 green chillies, seeded and sliced

1 tablespoon olive oil

1 tomato, chopped

½ green capsicum (pepper), thinly sliced

250 ml (8 fl oz) jar hot taco sauce

½ cup (125 ml/4 fl oz) chicken stock

8 olives, sliced

1 Cut end joint from chicken wings and discard.

2 Place onion, chillies and oil in a microwave-safe casserole, cover and cook on high 2 minutes.

3 Add chicken wings, tomato, capsicum, taco sauce, stock and olives. Stir well and arrange chicken with thickest parts near edge. Cover and cook on high 10 minutes, then on medium 15 minutes, or until tender, stirring after 7 minutes.

Serve with sour cream, rice and salad.

Mexican Salsa Chicken

Quick Meaty Mains

*T*he recipes in this chapter are selected mainly for today's busy lifestyle, but some are sufficiently impressive for entertaining. Choose good quality tender cuts of meat which are evenly sized, add interesting flavoursome ingredients, stop and test often rather than overcook and you will produce some tasty and impressive results to tempt the tastebuds.

FILLET OF BEEF WELLINGTON

TIME: 45 TO 47 MINUTES
SERVES 6 TO 8

1.5 kg (3 lb) middle cut fillet of beef in one piece

2 cloves garlic, peeled

2 tablespoons oil

¼ cup (60 ml/2 fl oz) brandy

2 sheets puff pastry

2 tablespoons French mustard

1 egg, beaten

1 Trim beef. Cut each clove of garlic in four. Make 4 small cuts in each side of beef and insert garlic. Tie roast at 5 cm (2 in) intervals with kitchen string. This holds the beef in

Recipes on previous pages: Magic Mince (page 59), Racks of Lamb with Minty Mustard Topping (page 54)

shape while browning. Cook in browning casserole on high 6 minutes.

2 Remove beef, add oil and cook on high 2 minutes. Return beef to casserole and cook on high 4 minutes, turning fillet four times during cooking for even browning. Cook on medium 20 minutes. Remove string.

3 Place brandy in a jug and cook on high 15 to 20 seconds to warm. Pour over fillet and ignite with flaming taper, let stand 5 minutes, turning beef twice. Leave to cool.

4 Place beef onto a sheet of puff pastry. Spread top and sides with French mustard. Brush edges of pastry with beaten egg and shape second sheet of pastry over beef. Seal edges and cut off excess pastry. Brush pastry with beaten egg and decorate with excess pastry.

Fillet of Beef Wellington

5 Bake in a convection microwave at 200°C (400°F) until pastry is well risen and golden.

Serve with mushroom sauce (see opposite page), Baby Buttered Potatoes (page 16), pumpkin and snow peas.

DEFROSTING MEAT

To defrost large pieces of beef, place on a roasting rack and cook on medium 5 to 8 minutes for each 500 g (1 lb). Defrosting steaks and chops takes only 3 to 4 minutes for each 500 g (1 lb) but should the meat start to brown while the centre is still frozen, cover the cooked sections with foil.

FILET MIGNON WITH MUSHROOM SAUCE

TIME: 21 TO 23 MINUTES
SERVES 4

4 filet mignon, 180 g (6 oz) each
15 g (½ oz) butter, melted

MUSHROOM SAUCE

15 g (½ oz) butter
125 g (4 oz) button mushrooms, sliced
1 tablespoon plain (all purpose) flour
300 ml (10 fl oz) canned beef consommé or beef stock
2 tablespoons cream
⅛ teaspoon salt
⅛ teaspoon pepper

1 Preheat a browning grill rack on high 9 minutes. Brush one side of each mignon with butter and place buttered side down on preheated grill. Cook on high 3 minutes.

2 Brush tops with butter and turn mignons over. Cook on high 3 minutes for rare.

3 To make sauce, place butter in a jug and heat on high 1 minute. Add mushrooms and cook 1 minute. Blend in flour. Cook a further minute on high. Stir in consommé and cook on high 3 to 4 minutes, stirring after 2 minutes.

4 Add cream and blend well. Season. Pour over filet mignons.

Serve accompanied with Jacket Potatoes (page 16) and salad.

Filet Mignon with Mushroom Sauce

Cooked Meat Defrosting and Reheating Chart

Food Type	Quantity	Power Setting	Time	Reheat Power Setting	Time	Standing Time
Casserole	750 ml (24 fl oz)	Defrost	20 mins	medium	10 to 12 mins	NA
	1.25 litre (40 fl oz)		30 mins		12 to 15 mins	NA
Meat Sauce	1 litre (32 fl oz)	"	30 to 35 mins	medium high	8 to 10 mins	NA
Lasagne	2 litre (64 fl oz)	"	40 to 45 mins (stand 10 mins halfway)	medium	40 to 45 mins (shield halfway)	10 mins
	single serve	"	5 mins	medium high	1 to 1½ mins	1 min
Meatloaf	1.5 litre (48 fl oz)	"	20 mins (shield and stand 5 mins halfway)	medium	10 mins (shield throughout)	5 mins
	1 slice (125 g/4 oz)	"	3 mins	medium high	1½ to 2 mins	1 min
	2 slices (250 g/8 oz)	"	5 mins		2 to 2½ mins	1 min
	4 slices (500 g/16 oz)	"	9 mins		3 to 3½ mins	1 to 2 mins
Meatballs in Sauce	1 litre (32 fl oz)	"	20 to 25 mins	medium high	8 to 10 mins	NA
Pre-browned Steaks	1 steak (100 g/3½ oz)	"	2½ to 3 mins	medium high	1 to 2 mins	1 to 2 mins
	2 steaks (200 g/7 oz)	"	4 to 5 mins		2 to 4 mins	1 to 2 mins
	4 steaks (400 g/14 oz)	"	6 to 7 mins		4 to 6 mins	1 to 2 mins
	6 steaks (600 g/21 oz)	"	8 to 9 mins		6 to 10 mins	2 to 3 mins
Pre-browned Chops	1 chop (100 g/3½ oz)	"	2 mins	medium high	1 min	1 min
	2 chops (200 g/7 oz)	"	3 mins		2 mins	1 min
	4 chops (400 g/14 oz)	"	4 mins		3 to 4 mins	1 to 2 mins
	6 chops (600 g/21 oz)	"	6 mins		5 to 6 mins	1 to 2 mins
Pre-browned Meat Patties	1 patty (125 g/4 oz)	"	3 to 4 mins	medium high	2 to 3 mins	1 min
	2 patties (250 g/8 oz)	"	5 to 6 mins		3 to 4 mins	1 min
	4 patties (500 g/16 oz)	"	9 to 10 mins		6 to 7 mins	1 to 2 mins
	6 patties (750 g/24 oz)	"	12 to 13 mins		8 to 10 mins	1 to 2 mins

Note: It is advisable to reheat food to an internal temperature of 70°C.

MARINATED BEEF

TIME: 30 TO 35 MINUTES
SERVES 8

1.5 to 2 kg (3 to 4 lb) whole fillet of beef

1 tablespoon wholegrain mustard

1 tablespoon oil

juice and rind of 1 lemon

1 tablespoon honey

½ teaspoon soy sauce

1 Trim beef. Combine mustard, oil, lemon juice and rind, honey and soy sauce. Coat fillet with mixture.

2 Cook fillet on a roasting (grilling) rack on medium-high 30 to 35 minutes. Turn once halfway through cooking. Stand covered with foil 15 minutes.

3 Slice beef and serve accompanied with Homemade Mustard (see below), Jacket Potatoes (page 16) and a green vegetable.

HOMEMADE MUSTARD

TIME: 2 MINUTES
MAKES 1½ CUPS
(375 ML/12 FL OZ)

1 cup mustard seeds

1 tablespoon whole black peppercorns

1 cup (250 ml/8 fl oz) olive oil

¼ cup (60 ml/2 fl oz) vermouth

¾ cup (185 ml/6 fl oz) white wine vinegar

½ tablespoon salt

½ teaspoon dried tarragon leaves

½ teaspoon dried dill

1 Place mustard seeds and peppercorns into blender. Blend 1 minute. Combine with remaining ingredients in a 1 litre (32 fl oz) casserole dish. Cover and cook on high 2 minutes.

2 Pour mustard mixture into sterilised jars. Seal. Allow to stand at least 24 hours before using.

Serve with beef or ham.

LEMON LAMB SATÉ

TIME: 14 MINUTES
SERVES 4

LEMON MARINADE

½ cup (125 ml/4 fl oz) lemon juice

½ cup (125 ml/4 fl oz) olive oil

2 cloves garlic, crushed

2 bay leaves

1 teaspoon chopped fresh oregano

½ teaspoon salt

¼ teaspoon freshly ground black pepper

LAMB

500 g (1 lb) lean lamb, cut into 2.5 cm (1 in) cubes

½ green capsicum (pepper) diced

1 medium onion, cut into eights, or 8 spring onions

1 lemon, cut into 8 wedges

4 bamboo saté sticks

1 Combine all marinade ingredients in a 2 litre (64 fl oz) bowl. Add lamb cubes and marinate for at least 1 hour or overnight.

2 Thread marinated lamb cubes and vegetables onto saté sticks. Place on a roasting (grilling) rack and cook on medium 6 minutes. Turn over and rearrange. Brush with remaining marinade. Cook 8 to 9 minutes.

Serve with lemon wedges. Accompany with Lemon Rice (page 70) and a green salad.

LAMB BURGERS

TIME: 12 MINUTES
SERVES 4

4 slices bacon

500 g (1 lb) minced lamb

½ cup finely chopped spring onions (shallots)

1½ teaspoons Worcestershire sauce

½ teaspoon mixed herbs

salt

4 slices cheddar cheese

1 Arrange bacon between two layers of white paper towel and cook on high 3 minutes.

2 Preheat a browning grill rack on high 5 minutes. Combine lamb, spring onions, sauce, herbs and salt and shape into 4 burgers. Place on preheated grill rack and cook on high 2 minutes. Top each burger with cheese.

3 Cut bacon slices in half and place 2 pieces on each patty. Cook on high 2 minutes for well done.

Serve on hot toasted buns with lettuce and tomato.

RACKS OF LAMB WITH MINTY MUSTARD TOPPING

TIME: 12 MINUTES
SERVES 2

> 2 racks of lamb with 4 cutlets per rack
> 30 g (1 oz) butter
> 1 onion, finely chopped
> 1 tablespoon mint jelly
> 1 tablespoon wholegrain mustard
> 1 egg white
> mint sprigs, to garnish

1 Trim as much fat as possible from racks of lamb. Heat a microwave browning casserole on high 3 minutes. Remove casserole with oven gloves, add butter and swirl around to cover base, then quickly place lamb in hot butter, meat side down, and allow to brown until butter stops sizzling.

2 Remove racks of lamb.

3 Stir onion into butter, cover and cook on high 2 minutes. Remove from microwave oven, stir in mint jelly and mustard, place in a bowl and leave to cool. Whisk egg white until stiff and fold into onion mixture.

4 Place racks of lamb in the browning casserole, meat upwards and spread minty mustard topping over in a thick layer. Cover and cook on high 2 minutes then on medium 5 minutes.

Serve garnished with mint, accompanied with new potatoes, glazed carrots and a green vegetable.

COOKING LAMB CHOPS

To cook 4 lamb chops (chops can be marinated in lemon juice, oil and garlic), cook in a preheated browning casserole on one side on high for 1 minute, then turn and cook the other side, also on high, for 3 to 4 minutes.

SWEET AND SOUR PORK CASSEROLE

TIME: 35 MINUTES
SERVES 6

> 750 g (1½ lb) lean pork shoulder, cut into 2 cm (¾ in) pieces
> 2 tablespoons seasoned cornflour
> 3 tablespoons soy sauce
> ¼ cup (45 g/1½ oz) brown sugar
> ¼ cup (60 ml/2 fl oz) vinegar
> ¼ teaspoon ground ginger
> 440 g (14 oz) can pineapple pieces in juice
> 1 onion, chopped
> 1 stalk celery, chopped
> 1 clove garlic, finely chopped
> ½ red and ½ green capsicum (pepper), chopped

1 Toss pork in seasoned cornflour in a 2 litre (64 fl oz) casserole dish. Add remaining ingredients except capsicum.

2 Cover and cook on high 5 minutes. Reduce power to medium and cook 20 minutes, stirring twice during cooking.

3 Add capsicum, adjust seasonings and thickening if necessary and continue cooking on medium 10 minutes.

Serve with rice or noodles.

SPICY PORK RIBS

TIME: 20 MINUTES
SERVES 4

> 750 g (1½ lb) pork spareribs
> 1 onion, chopped
> 2 tablespoons soy sauce
> 3 tablespoons honey
> 2 tablespoons fresh lemon juice
> 1 clove garlic, crushed
> ¼ teaspoon salt
> pinch pepper
> ½ teaspoon curry powder
> ¼ teaspoon chilli powder
> ½ teaspoon ground ginger
> 3 tablespoons oil

1 Remove rind and excess fat from ribs. Combine remaining ingredients for marinade. Prick pork with skewer and place into marinade for 2 hours.

2 Place ribs onto a roasting (grilling) browning rack and cook on high 20 minutes, turning after 10 minutes. Spareribs may also be cooked in an oven bag.

Serve with Rice Pilaf (page 69) or Saffron Brown Rice (page 70) and salad.

SPICY CHICKEN WINGS

Chicken wings can also be cooked with the same method as the Spicy Pork Ribs.

Combine pork, onion, basil and oil

Add mushrooms

PORK AND MUSHROOM STROGANOFF

TIME: 30 MINUTES
SERVES 4 TO 6

500 g (1 lb) pork fillet, cut in strips

1 onion, peeled and sliced

½ teaspoon chopped fresh basil

3 tablespoons oil

125 g (4 oz) button mushrooms, sliced

2 tablespoons cornflour

salt and pepper to taste

1 cup (250 ml/8 fl oz) chicken stock

1¼ cups (300 ml/10 fl oz) sour cream

1 tablespoon chopped parsley

Pork and Mushroom Stroganoff

1 Place pork, onion, basil and 1 tablespoon oil in a shallow dish. Cover and cook on medium-high 10 minutes, stirring once.

2 Add mushrooms and cook a further 5 minutes on medium. Set aside.

3 Combine rest of oil, cornflour, salt, pepper and stock in glass jug. Cook on high 3 to 5 minutes. Stir vigorously when cooked. Fold through pork mixture. Cover and cook on medium 5 minutes.

4 Add sour cream and parsley. Stir through evenly. Cook uncovered on medium 5 minutes.

Serve hot with rice or noodles.

Add oil, cornflour, stock and seasonings

Combine seasoned breadcrumbs, Parmesan cheese, herbs and seasonings

Coat veal with egg and then crumb mixture

Arrange veal in shallow dish and add tomato mixture and mozzarella cheese

VEAL SCALOPPINE

TIME: 22 MINUTES
SERVES 4

- 4 veal steaks
- ¼ cup (30 g/1 oz) dry breadcrumbs
- ⅓ cup (45 g/1½ oz) Parmesan cheese
- 1 tablespoon chopped parsley
- salt and pepper to taste
- 1 teaspoon chopped fresh basil
- 1 egg, beaten
- 2 large tomatoes
- 125 g (4 oz) mozzarella cheese, grated

1 Pound veal steaks and slice in half. Combine breadcrumbs, 1 tablespoon Parmesan cheese, parsley, salt, pepper and basil. Dip veal in egg and coat with crumb mixture.

2 Place veal on a microwave roasting (grilling) rack. Cook on medium-high uncovered 10 to 12 minutes, turning once.

3 Slice tomatoes. Layer veal steaks, tomato and mozzarella cheese in a shallow dish. Sprinkle with remaining Parmesan cheese. Cook on medium-high 10 minutes.

Serve hot with a green salad or a green vegetable.

VEAL MOZZARELLA

TIME: 22 MINUTES
SERVES 4

SAUCE

- 250 g (8 oz) tomato paste
- ¼ teaspoon dried oregano
- ½ teaspoon dried basil
- ¼ teaspoon garlic salt
- ½ teaspoon sugar
- ⅛ teaspoon white pepper

VEAL

- 4 veal steaks
- ¾ cup grated mozzarella cheese
- 1 tablespoon finely chopped parsley

1 Combine all sauce ingredients in a medium-sized bowl and cook on high 2 minutes. Reduce power to medium and cook 6 minutes. Set aside.

2 Place veal in a single layer in baking dish and cook on medium 8 to 9 minutes. Drain.

3 Spoon sauce over veal. Sprinkle with cheese and parsley and cook on medium 6 to 7 minutes until cheese melts.

Serve with spinach fettuccine and a green salad.

STIR YOUR SAUCE

Stirring sauce during cooking ensures an even distribution of the cooked sauce and ensures a thoroughly tasty meal.

Veal Mozzarella

Combine lemon juice, egg yolks, and seasonings

Add melted butter and whisk

Cook on defrost stirring every 30–45 seconds

VEAL WITH AVOCADO AND HOLLANDAISE SAUCE

TIME: 17 MINUTES
SERVES 6

HOLLANDAISE SAUCE

- 100 g (3 oz) butter
- 3 egg yolks
- 2 tablespoons fresh lemon juice or white wine or tarragon vinegar
- salt and pepper to taste

VEAL

- 1 tablespoon oil
- 6 veal steaks
- 1 large ripe avocado, peeled and sliced

Veal with Avocado and Hollandaise Sauce

1 To prepare sauce, place butter in bowl and melt on high 1 minute. Beat together egg yolks, lemon juice, salt and pepper and stir into the melted butter. Cook on defrost 4 minutes, stirring every 30 to 45 seconds. Beat sauce while it cools. Sauce will thicken on cooling.

2 Preheat browning dish on high 4 minutes. Add oil and cook veal fillets, 3 at a time, on high 4 minutes, turning after 2 minutes. Repeat for remaining fillets.

Serve veal topped with avocado slices and hollandaise sauce, accompanied with Lemon Rice (page 70) and a green vegetable.

MAGIC MINCE

TIME: 21 MINUTES
SERVES 4

1 onion, chopped
1 clove garlic, crushed
2 tablespoons vegetable oil
500 g (1 lb) finely minced beef
1 carrot, grated
4 tablespoons tomato paste

410 g (13 oz) can tomatoes
1 beef stock cube, crumbled
pepper to taste
3 tablespoons chopped parsley

1 Place onion, garlic and oil in a microwave browning casserole, cover and cook on high 2 minutes.

2 Stir in mince, arrange in an even layer, cover and cook on high 4 minutes, stirring after 2 minutes.

3 Add remaining ingredients, except parsley, and stir well. Cover and cook on high 15 minutes or until tender. Stir in parsley.

Serve with pasta or rice, in tacos, crêpes or cabbage rolls or use as a stuffing mixture for vegetables such as capsicum (pepper), eggplant (aubergine) or marrow.

Magic Mince

MICROWAVING MINI ROASTS OF LAMB

1 Weigh the lamb to calculate cooking time by allowing 1 minute for every 100 g for Eye of Loin or 1½ minutes fo other cuts. Add extra time as per the chart according to your microwave wattage.

2 Place lamb on an upturned saucer in a microwave roasting dish. Brush with combined soy sauce and honey. Cook for calculated time, brushing with glaze throughout.

3 Lamb should still feel springy. Remove from microwave. Cover with foil and 'stand' as per chart to complete cooking. Lamb should feel firmer.

Note: If cooking more than one roast, do individually for best results.

MEXICAN TACOS

TIME: 20 ½ MINUTES
SERVES 4 TO 5

500 g (1 lb) minced beef
1 onion, finely chopped
2 tablespoons oil
3 tablespoons tomato paste
1 teaspoon mixed herbs
½ teaspoon chilli powder

Lamb Mini Roast Cooking Times Chart

Cut	Microwave Wattage	Power Setting	Total Cooking Time (Per 100 g + Extra)	Standing Time
Topside and Round	750 W	Medium high	1½ mins + Nil	Double total cooking time
	700 W	Medium high	1½ mins + 30 secs	Double total cooking time
	650 W	Medium high	1½ mins + 1½ mins	Double total cooking time
	600 W	Medium high	1½ mins + 2 mins	Double total cooking time
Eye of Loin	750 W	Medium high	1 min + Nil	2 mins
	700 W	Medium high	1 min + 30 secs	2 mins
	650 W	Medium high	1 min + 1 min	2 mins
	600 W	Medium high	1 min + 1½ mins	2 mins

Oven Bag Roasting Chart

Cut	Degree of Cooking	Mins Per 500 g	Internal Temp	Standing Time	Internal Temp on Standing	Power Setting
BEEF Blade Rolled Skirt Brisket (boned and rolled) Round Silverside	Medium Well done	14 to 16 18 to 20	55°C 65°C	10 to 15 mins	60 to 65°C 70 to 75°C	Medium low
VEAL Shoulder (boned and rolled)	Well done	16 to 18	70°C	10 to 15 mins	75 to 80°C	Medium low
LAMB Shoulder (boned and rolled)	Medium Well done	16 to 18 18 to 20	60°C 70°C	10 to 15 mins	70°C 75 to 80°C	Medium low

1 green chilli, finely chopped

salt and pepper to taste

dash tabasco sauce

dash cayenne pepper

8 to 10 taco shells

1 lettuce, shredded

2 tomatoes, chopped

½ cup (60 g/2 oz) grated cheddar cheese

1¼ cups (300 ml/10 fl oz) sour cream

1 Place beef, onion, oil, tomato paste, mixed herbs, chilli powder, green chilli, salt, pepper, tabasco sauce and cayenne pepper into a shallow casserole. Cover and cook on high 10 minutes, stirring twice.

2 Uncover and cook on medium 10 minutes. Set aside.

3 Place 8 to 10 taco shells upside down on microwave turntable. Cook on high 30 seconds.

4 Serve taco shells filled with lettuce, tomato, meat mixture, sprinkled with cheese and a spoonful of sour cream.

Serve for a quick light meal, followed with a salad.

CALF LIVER AND BACON WITH MUSTARD CREAM

TIME: 16 MINUTES
SERVES 4

375 g (12 oz) calf's liver

4 large bacon rashers

1 small onion, finely chopped

½ teaspoon freshly ground pepper

¼ teaspoon salt

3 tablespoons sweet vermouth

1 tablespoon tomato paste

1 teaspoon cornflour

3 tablespoons beef consommé or beef stock

MUSTARD CREAM

1 cup (250 ml/8 fl oz) light sour cream

3 tablespoons French mustard

1 Soak liver in cold, salted water for 10 minutes. Remove skin and cut liver into thin slices. Derind bacon rashers and cut each rasher into 2.5 cm (1 in) lengths.

2 Place bacon and onion in casserole and cook on high 4 minutes, stirring after 2 minutes. Add liver and cook on high 2 minutes. Add freshly ground pepper and salt, vermouth and tomato paste.

Calf's Liver and Bacon

3 Blend in cornflour and consommé. Cover and cook on medium 10 minutes, stirring and rearranging liver every 3 minutes.

4 To make mustard cream, blend sour cream and French mustard.

Serve with mustard cream, accompanied with Baby Buttered Potatoes (page 16) and Baby Squash Provencal (page 17).

Popular Pasta and Rice

*P*asta and rice dishes are always popular because they are versatile and quick and easy to prepare. The most convenient way to cook rice is in the microwave oven. Pasta can be cooked in the microwave but it is often quicker to prepare a sauce in the microwave while cooking the pasta on the stovetop. There are a large variety of delicious menu choices.

CHINESE RAVIOLI

TIME: 20 OR 35 MINUTES
MAKES 30

250 g (8 oz) pork mince

125 g (4 oz) raw prawn meat, minced

4 dried mushrooms, soaked in warm water for 20 minutes and finely chopped

1 spring onion (shallot), finely chopped

1 tablespoon soy sauce

½ teaspoon sesame oil

1 egg yolk, beaten

30 dim sim pastry sheets

1 egg white

6 to 8 cups (1.5 to 2 litres/ 48 to 64 fl oz) boiling water

3 tablespoons oil

1 Combine pork, prawn meat, mushrooms and spring onion in a small bowl. Mix in soy sauce, sesame oil and beaten egg yolk so that the mixture resembles a thick paste.

2 Place 1 teaspoon of filling into centre of each pastry sheet. Brush edges with egg white. Fold over pastry to form a triangle or fold opposite corners together. Press edges to seal.

Steamed method: Pour boiling water into a large casserole. Add half the triangles, cover and cook on medium 10 minutes. Drain and repeat with remaining triangles.

Fried method: Preheat browning dish on high 5 minutes. Add oil and cook in batches of 6 on high 4 to 6 minutes, turning once while each batch is cooking.

Serve with sweet chilli sauce.

Recipes on previous pages: Lemon Rice (page 70), Tomato and Basil Penne (page 64), Pasta and Broccoli Salad (page 68)

SAUCE FOR PASTA

Use a good quality processed napolitana or similar tomato-based pasta sauce for the best flavour.

FETTUCCINE CARBONARA

TIME: 4 MINUTES
SERVES 2 TO 4

4 rashers bacon

250 g (8 oz) fettuccine, freshly cooked

⅔ cup (150 ml/5 fl oz) cream

2 eggs

½ cup (60 g/2 oz) grated Parmesan cheese

parsley, to garnish

1 Cook bacon between 2 sheets of paper towelling on high 4 minutes. Chop bacon.

2 Place hot pasta in bowl, add cream, beaten eggs, cheese and chopped bacon. Toss through pasta.

Garnish with chopped parsley and serve immediately accompanied with a green salad.

COOKING BACON

Cook bacon rashers between sheets of white paper towel as this will absorb the fat, prevent spattering and keep oven walls clean.

TOMATO AND BASIL PENNE

TIME: 10 MINUTES
SERVES 4

2 cups penne pasta

1 large onion, finely chopped

2 tablespoons olive oil

2 cups diced eggplant (aubergine)

2 cups (500 ml/16 fl oz) napolitana sauce

½ cup shredded fresh basil

grated Parmesan cheese, to serve

1 Cook penne pasta on the stovetop in a large pan of boiling salted water until tender, about 10 minutes.

2 Meanwhile place onion and oil in a microwave browning casserole, cover and cook on high 2 minutes.

3 Stir in eggplant and cook covered on high 4 minutes, stirring after 2 minutes.

4 Stir in napolitana sauce and basil and cook on high for 4 minutes or until hot. Serve sauce over freshly cooked, drained pasta. Sprinkle with grated Parmesan cheese.

Accompany with a green salad.

CONVENTIONAL TIME-SAVER

If you are preparing a large meal it can be more efficient to cook the pasta conventionally on the stovetop, while you use the microwave for sauces and other dishes.

Fettuccine Carbonara

SAVOURY LASAGNE

TIME: 31 MINUTES
SERVES 8

   8 sheets short lasagne

   2 cups (500 ml/16 fl oz) boiling
      water

   ½ teaspoon salt

   810 g (30 oz) can whole peeled
      tomatoes, chopped

   ½ teaspoon dried basil

   250 g (8 oz) peperoni sausage,
      sliced

   1 onion, finely chopped

   1 clove garlic, crushed

   freshly ground black pepper

   250 g (8 oz) ricotta cheese

   2 eggs, beaten

   ½ cup (125 ml/4 fl oz) cream

   250 g (8 oz) mozzarella cheese,
      grated

   ¼ cup grated Parmesan cheese

1 Place 4 sheets lasagne in a shallow dish, add boiling water and salt. Cover with plastic wrap and cook on high 4 minutes. Carefully lift out pasta and allow to drain. Cook remaining lasagne on high 4 minutes and drain.

2 Mix together tomatoes, basil, peperoni sausage, onion, garlic and black pepper and set aside.

3 Combine ricotta cheese, eggs and cream in a glass jug. Cook on high 3 minutes, stirring twice.

4 Starting with lasagne sheets, arrange lasagne, tomato and sausage mixture and ricotta sauce in layers in a greased shallow dish. Sprinkle ricotta layer with grated mozzarella and Parmesan cheeses. Top with ricotta mix and Parmesan cheese.

5 Cook on medium-high

10 minutes, then on medium 10 minutes. Stand 5 minutes uncovered.

Serve hot, accompanied with a green salad.

RIGATONI WITH RED CORIANDER PESTO

TIME: 6 TO 10 MINUTES
SERVES 2

   200 g (6½ oz) rigatoni

   1 large red capsicum (pepper),
      finely chopped

   4 spring onions (shallots), thinly
      sliced

   2 tablespoons olive oil

   ¼ cup pine nuts

   2 cloves garlic, crushed

   1 cup fresh coriander leaves

   2 tablespoons tomato paste

   ½ cup (60 g/2 oz) grated
      Parmesan cheese

   extra grated Parmesan cheese,
      to serve

1 Cook rigatoni in a pan of boiling salted water for 10 minutes. Meanwhile place capsicum, spring onions, oil, pine nuts and garlic into a microwave-safe casserole.

2 Cover and cook on high 4 minutes. Stir in coriander, tomato paste and cheese, cover and cook on medium 2 minutes.

Serve sauce over freshly cooked, drained rigatoni. Sprinkle with extra grated Parmesan cheese.

FETTUCCINE WITH CALAMARI SAUCE

TIME: 10 TO 22 MINUTES
SERVES 2 TO 4

FETTUCCINE

   4 cups (1 litre/32 fl oz) boiling
      water

   1 teaspoon salt

   1 tablespoon oil

   250 g (8 oz) fettuccine

CALAMARI SAUCE

   125 g (4 oz) calamari, cleaned
      and sliced

   1 tablespoon chopped parsley

   6 spring onions (shallots),
      chopped

   juice of 1 lemon

   freshly ground black pepper

   ½ cup (125 ml/4 fl oz) white wine

   2 tablespoons sour cream

   grated Parmesan cheese, to serve

1 Place boiling water, salt and oil into a 2 litre (64 fl oz) casserole dish. Add fettuccine, cover and cook on high 15 minutes. Stir and set aside. Alternatively cook fettuccine on the stovetop in a pan of boiling salted water for 10 minutes.

2 Combine sauce ingredients, except for sour cream, in a shallow dish. Cover and cook on high 5 to 7 minutes. Blend in sour cream.

3 Drain fettuccine, add sauce and serve with Parmesan cheese, accompanied with a green salad.

Savoury Lasagne

VEGERONI WITH ASPARAGUS MACADAMIA SAUCE

TIME: 7 TO 10 MINUTES
SERVES 4

3 cups vegeroni

1 onion, finely chopped

30 g (1 oz) butter

310 g (10 oz) can asparagus cuts, drained

½ cup (60 g/2 oz) macadamia nuts, roasted and ground

1 cup (250 ml/8 fl oz) cream

½ cup (60 g/2 oz) grated Parmesan cheese

extra grated Parmesan cheese, to serve

1 Cook vegeroni on the stovetop in a large pan of boiling, salted water for 10 minutes.

2 Meanwhile place onion and butter in a microwave safe casserole, cover and cook on high 2 minutes.

3 Stir in asparagus, nuts and cream and cook covered on high 4 to 5 minutes or until hot.

4 Stir in grated Parmesan cheese. Serve over freshly cooked, drained vegeroni. Sprinkle with extra grated Parmesan cheese.

PASTA AND BROCCOLI SALAD

TIME: 13 TO 18 MINUTES
SERVES 8

250 g (8 oz) pasta

4 cups (1 litre/32 fl oz) boiling water

1 teaspoon salt

250 g (8 oz) broccoli, cut in florets

1 tomato, chopped

3 tablespoons olive oil

freshly ground black pepper

½ teaspoon dried basil

2 tablespoons grated Parmesan cheese

1 Place pasta, boiling water and salt in a 4 litre (128 fl oz) casserole dish. Cover and cook on high 15 minutes. Alternatively, cook on the stovetop in a pan of rapidly boiling, salted water for 10 minutes. Set aside.

2 Place broccoli in a shallow dish. Cover and cook on high 3 minutes. Combine broccoli with tomato, olive oil, pepper and basil.

3 Drain pasta. Toss broccoli and pasta together. Sprinkle with Parmesan cheese.

Serve with fish, chicken or veal or as part of a buffet party menu.

CRUNCHY TUNA PIE

TIME: 20 MINUTES
SERVES 6 TO 8

125 g (4 oz) pasta noodles

4 cups (1 litre/32 fl oz) boiling water

½ teaspoon salt

125 g (4 oz) cheddar cheese, grated

⅔ cup (160 ml/5 fl oz) sour cream

4 hard-boiled eggs, chopped

1 teaspoon tomato paste

425 g (14 oz) can tuna, drained and flaked

salt and pepper to taste

75 g (2½ oz) packet potato chips (crisps)

1 Place noodles, water and salt into a 2 litre (64 fl oz) casserole dish. Cover and cook on high 10 minutes. Stand for 10 minutes. Drain noodles.

2 Combine with cheddar cheese, sour cream, hard-boiled eggs, tomato paste, tuna, salt and pepper.

3 Place mixture in a shallow microwave-safe baking dish. Top with potato chips. Cook uncovered on medium 10 minutes.

Serve hot, accompanied with a green salad and garlic bread.

TURKEY CHOW MEIN

TIME: 18 MINUTES
SERVES 4 TO 8

2 boned turkey thighs, diced into 2 cm (¾ in) pieces

1 to 2 tablespoons cornflour

½ cup (125 ml/4 fl oz) rich chicken stock

1½ tablespoons soy sauce

1 cup thinly sliced celery

1 onion, diced

440 g (14 oz) can Chinese mixed vegetables, drained

250 g (8 oz) mushrooms, sliced

1 packet chow mein noodles, freshly cooked

1 Place turkey pieces in a casserole. Cover and cook on high 6 to 8 minutes, stirring after 3 minutes.

2 Blend cornflour and stock and add to casserole.

3 Stir in soy sauce and vegetables. Cover and cook on high 12 minutes, stirring after 6 minutes.

Serve surrounded by chow mein noodles.

Combine rice, butter, onion and garlic

Add boiling stock

Lightly fork through ham, peas, capsicum and seasoning.

Rice Pilaf

RICE PILAF

TIME: 12 MINUTES
SERVES 4 TO 6

15 g (½ oz) butter

1 small onion, finely chopped

1 clove garlic, finely chopped

1 cup long grain rice, washed

1 ¾ cups (430 ml/14 fl oz) boiling chicken stock

¼ cup diced ham

¼ cup small cooked prawns, optional

1 cup cooked peas

½ red capsicum (pepper), diced

½ green capsicum (pepper), diced

salt to taste

ground pepper

2 tablespoons toasted flaked almonds

toasted sesame seeds, to garnish

1 Place butter, onion and garlic into a deep casserole dish. Cover and cook on high 3 minutes.

2 Add rice and cook 1 minute. Add boiling stock. Cover and cook on high 8 minutes. Let stand 4 minutes.

3 Lightly fork in ham, prawns if used, peas, capsicum and seasonings and sprinkle with toasted almonds and sesame seeds.

WHITE RICE

TIME: 8 MINUTES
SERVES 4 TO 6

1 cup long or short grain rice, washed

1¾ cups (430 ml/14 fl oz) boiling water

15 g (½ oz) butter

½ teaspoon salt

1 Place all ingredients in a 1 litre (32 fl oz) casserole dish. Cover and cook on high 8 minutes. Let stand 4 minutes before serving.

BROWN RICE

TIME: 22 MINUTES
SERVES 4 TO 6

1 cup brown rice, washed

2 cups (500 ml/16 fl oz) boiling water

15 g (½ oz) butter

⅛ teaspoon salt

1 Place all ingredients in a 2 litre (64 fl oz) casserole dish. Cook on high 22 minutes. Let stand 5 minutes before serving.

KEEPING RICE HOT

Cooked rice will remain hot in a covered casserole dish for 10 minutes at room temperature. Take advantage of this time to cook or reheat accompanying food.

REHEATING RICE

Cold cooked rice can be reheated on high. Add 1 tablespoon of warm water to rice, cover and heat 2 to 3 minutes.

LEMON RICE

TIME: 10 MINUTES
SERVES 4 TO 6

15 g (½ oz) butter

1 cup long grain rice, washed

⅛ teaspoon cumin seeds

⅛ teaspoon coriander seeds

¼ teaspoon salt

½ teaspoon ground turmeric

1¾ cups (430 ml/14 fl oz) boiling water

juice of 1 lemon

chopped coriander leaves, to garnish

1 Place butter in a 2 litre (64 fl oz) casserole dish and cook on high 1 minute. Add rice, cumin, coriander seeds, salt and turmeric and cook on high 1 minute.

2 Stir in boiling water and cook on high 8 minutes. Let stand 4 minutes.

3 Add strained lemon juice, forking in lightly. Sprinkle with coriander.

Serve with fish, chicken or lamb, or with a spicy, curried main course dish.

SAFFRON BROWN RICE

TIME: 31 MINUTES
SERVES 4 TO 6

1 cup brown rice, washed

1 small onion, chopped

15 g (½ oz) butter

1 chicken or vegetable stock cube, crumbled

½ teaspoon salt

⅛ teaspoon saffron powder

ground pepper

1¼ cups (300 ml/10 fl oz) water

½ cup (125 ml/4 fl oz) dry white wine

1 Place rice, onion, butter, chicken cube, salt, saffron and pepper into a deep microwave-safe casserole dish.

2 Combine water and wine in a bowl and cook on high 5 minutes until boiling. Pour over rice, cover and cook on high 26 minutes.

3 Let stand covered 10 minutes to complete cooking.

Serve with a fish, chicken or vegetable dish.

SPICY RICE WITH PEAS

TIME: 15 MINUTES
SERVES 4 TO 6

30 g (1 oz) butter

1 teaspoon cumin seeds

½ teaspoon dry crushed chilli or ⅛ teaspoon chilli powder

½ teaspoon ground pepper

1 cup short grain rice, washed

½ teaspoon ground turmeric

1 teaspoon salt

1 cup peas

1¾ cups (430 ml/14 fl oz) boiling water or stock

1 Place butter into a large microwave-safe casserole dish. Cook on high 1 minute.

2 Add cumin seeds, chilli and pepper and cook 1 minute more. Add washed rice, turmeric and salt and cook on high 1 minute. Add peas and boiling water or stock. Cover.

3 Place casserole on a large plate to collect any spillovers. Cook on high 10 to 12 minutes, until tender. Stand 4 minutes, then fork rice up lightly.

Serve hot as an accompaniment to Asian-style main courses.

PARSLEY RICE RING

TIME: 6 MINUTES
SERVES 6

- 125 g (4 oz) butter
- 2 tablespoons finely chopped onion
- 1 cup finely chopped parsley
- 3 cups cooked rice (1 cup raw)
- 3 eggs, separated

1 Place butter into a 2 litre (64 fl oz) bowl and cook on high 2 minutes. Add onion, parsley, rice and egg yolks and blend together.

2 Fold in stiffly beaten egg whites and pour mixture into a greased microwave-safe ring dish. Level top of mixture with a spoon and cook on high 4 minutes.

3 Unmould onto a round platter to serve. Centre may be filled with various fillings such as cooked vegetables or a salad.

Add onion, parsley, rice and egg yolks to melted butter

Fold egg whites into rice mixture

Spoon mixture into greased ring dish

Speedy
Snacks

*T*he microwave oven
has helped change
many traditional eating
patterns. This chapter has
a collection of speedy
snacks for 'grazers' or
people who eat at odd
times of the day and for
those who have to eat in
a hurry because of
commitments in their
busy life. It is made up of
drinks, sandwiches,
snacks, light meals and
breakfast dishes — all of
which are quick and
simple to prepare.

CHOCOLATE THICK SHAKE

TIME: 1 MINUTE
SERVES 2

> 3 large scoops chocolate ice cream
>
> 3 tablespoons milk
>
> 2 tablespoons chocolate syrup
>
> 4 whole marshmallows
>
> 2 tablespoons whipped cream

1 Place all ingredients into a large glass or jug. Cook on medium 1 minute, stirring twice during cooking.

2 Pour into 2 glasses. Top with whipped cream.

HOT MOCHA CHOCOLATE

TIME: 8 MINUTES
SERVES 4 TO 6

> 50 g (2 oz) cocoa
>
> 30 g (1 oz) instant coffee
>
> 4 to 6 teaspoons coffee crystals
>
> 4 cups (1 litre/32 fl oz) hot water
>
> whipped cream
>
> chocolate curls

1 Combine cocoa, coffee and coffee crystals. Heat water in a jug on high 8 minutes until almost boiling. Stir in coffee mixture.

2 Pour into serving cups, top with whipped cream and chocolate curls and serve.

Recipes on previous pages: Crostata with Brie and Artichokes (page 77), Salami and Pickle Bagel (page 74)

CAPPUCCINO

TIME: 2 TO 3 MINUTES
SERVES 2

> 2 to 3 teaspoons brown sugar or coffee crystals
>
> 2 teaspoons instant coffee
>
> 1⅓ cups (330 ml/11 fl oz) hot water
>
> ¼ cup (60 ml/2 fl oz) orange liqueur
>
> whipped cream
>
> cocoa

1 In a jug, combine sugar, instant coffee and hot water. Cover and cook on high 2 to 3 minutes until boiling.

2 Stir to dissolve sugar then mix in liqueur.

3 Pour into coffee cups and top with whipped cream. Sprinkle lightly with cocoa.

IRISH COFFEE

TIME: 13 MINUTES
SERVES 6 TO 8

> ¼ cup brown sugar or coffee crystals
>
> 9 teaspoons instant coffee
>
> 5½ cups (1.4 litres/44 fl oz) water
>
> 1½ cups (375 ml/12 fl oz) Irish whisky
>
> whipped cream
>
> cinnamon sugar

1 In a 2 litre (64 fl oz) jug, combine sugar, instant coffee and water and cook on high 13 minutes or until very hot.

2 Stir in whisky and pour into individual cups. Top with cream and sprinkle lightly with cinnamon sugar.

SALAMI AND PICKLE BAGEL

TIME: 2 MINUTES
SERVES 1

> 1 bagel
>
> 3 thin slices salami
>
> 1 large slice tomato
>
> 1 dill pickled cucumber, sliced diagonally
>
> 1 pickled onion, thinly sliced, optional
>
> 1 slice cheddar cheese

1 Slice bagel in half to make two rings. Layer salami, tomato, pickles and cheese on bottom half. Cover with top half.

2 Wrap in clear plastic wrap and heat in microwave on defrost 2 minutes until warm and cheese has melted.

Eat straight away for a hearty snack or satisfying lunch.

WARMING SLICED BREAD AND DINNER ROLLS

Arrange 6 dinner rolls or 6 slices of bread in a napkin-lined bread basket and microwave on high 15 seconds. Warm uncut French and garlic bread on high 30 seconds. Avoid overheating.

FELAFEL BEAN ROLL

TIME: 1 MINUTE
SERVES 1

  1 wholemeal pita pocket bread

  2 tablespoons hummus or chick pea dip

  ⅓ cup canned kidney beans, rinsed and drained

  2 tablespoons tabbouleh salad

1 Slit around circumference of pocket bread, leaving about 2.5 cm (1 in) attached, and open out to form a single layer.

2 Spread thickest half with hummus, sprinkle kidney beans over and top with salad. Roll up covered half from open side to joined side and continue

Cheese and Ham Loaf

rolling until the thinner layer is wrapped around the roll.

3 Wrap in greaseproof paper and heat in microwave on high 1 minute.

Eat immediately for a healthy snack.

CAMEMBERT, BRIE

To warm: place 250 g (8 oz) cheese on plate. Cook on medium-low 30 to 40 seconds. Let stand 5 minutes before serving.

CHEESE AND HAM LOAF

TIME: 2 MINUTES
SERVES 8 TO 10

  1 stick French bread

  8 to 10 slices Swiss cheese

  8 to 10 sliced cooked ham

1 Slice French bread into 8 to 10 portions to within 1 cm (½ in) of base. Between each slice place 1 slice cheese and 1 slice ham.

2 Place loaf into a serving basket. Cook on high 1 to 2 minutes. Cheese will melt.

Serve cut into slices.

SPICY SALSA RICE

TIME: 2 MINUTES
SERVES 1

    1 cup cooked rice

    2 tablespoons salsa dip

    1 tablespoon light sour cream

1 Mix all ingredients together with a fork in a soup bowl or pasta bowl. Cover with clear plastic wrap and microwave on medium 2 minutes.

Serve for a quick tasty snack.

LEFT-OVER RICE

Use rice that has been left-over from another meal for this snack.

LEFT-OVER PASTA

Use pasta noodles that have been left from a previous meal for this snack.

SEAFOOD NOODLES

TIME: 2 MINUTES
SERVES 1

    1 cup cooked pasta

    2 tablespoons taramasalata dip

    1 tablespoon light sour cream

    2 teaspoons French dressing

1 Mix all ingredients together with a plastic spoon or spatula in a pasta bowl or soup bowl. Cover with clear plastic wrap and microwave on medium 2 minutes.

Serve for a speedy satisfying snack.

SHORTCUT MEXICAN PIZZA

TIME: 3 MINUTES
SERVES 1 TO 2

    1 round of Lebanese pita bread

    ½ cup (25 ml/4 fl oz) taco sauce

    2 tablespoons chopped parsley

    ½ cup grated cheddar cheese

    ½ cup grated mozzarella cheese

    2 teaspoons minced chillies

    1 tomato, thinly sliced

1 Place bread on the turntable of the microwave oven, spread with the taco sauce and sprinkle with parsley.

2 Mix grated cheese with minced chillies and sprinkle evenly over the taco sauce. Arrange tomato slices in a ring on top of cheese. Cook on high 3 minutes.

Serve immediately cut into wedges.

PIRI PIRI CASHEWS

TIME: 5 ½ MINUTES
SERVES 4 TO 6

    2 teaspoons butter

    185 g (6 oz) unsalted cashews

    ½ teaspoon cayenne pepper

    ½ teaspoon salt

    dash nutmeg

1 Melt butter in a mixing bowl on high 30 seconds. Add cashews, stirring until coated with butter. Cook 5 minutes on high. Drain on kitchen paper towels.

2 Combine cayenne pepper, salt and nutmeg and sprinkle over cashews. Serve with drinks or as a party snack.

PORK BALLS WITH DIPPING SAUCE

TIME: 10 MINUTES
MAKES 48

    375 g (12 oz) minced pork

    1 cup (60 g/2 oz) fresh breadcrumbs

    ¼ cup (30 g/1 oz) grated Parmesan cheese

    1 tablespoon finely chopped parsley

    ⅛ teaspoon cayenne pepper

    2 eggs, beaten

1 Crumble pork into a bowl and cook on high 4 minutes, stirring after 2 minutes. Drain well. Blend in remaining ingredients.

2 Using a teaspoon, shape mixture into small balls. Chill for 15 minutes.

Line a 30 cm (12 in) plate with paper towel and place 24 balls evenly around the edge. Cook on high 3 minutes or until firm and heated through. Repeat with remaining balls.

Serve with Dipping Sauce for a simple-to-make party savoury.

DIPPING SAUCE

1 tablespoon wholegrain mustard
½ cup (125 ml/4 fl oz) natural yoghurt
Blend mustard with yoghurt. Serve in a small bowl.

MEAT BALLS

Roll meat balls with wet hands to prevent sticking.

EGGS EN COCOTTE

TIME: 2 MINUTES
SERVES 2

2 large eggs

2 tablespoons cream

2 thin slices butter

freshly ground black pepper

ground rock salt

*2 teaspoons grated cheese,
optional*

1 Crack eggs into 2 individual
buttered cocotte or small soufflé
dishes. Top gently with cream,
butter and seasonings. Sprinkle with
cheese if desired.

2 Place in north and south positions
on edge of microwave turntable and
cook on defrost 2 minutes.

3 Serve for a light but nourishing
breakfast, accompanied with toast
and fruit juice.

VARIATIONS

You may put chopped herbs, ham,
chicken, mushrooms or tomatoes at
the bottom of the dish.

MUSHROOMS ON TOAST

TIME: 1 MINUTE
SERVES 2

*125 g (4 oz) button mushrooms,
sliced*

2 teaspoons butter

juice of 1 lemon

4 cherry tomatoes, cut in wedges

freshly ground pepper

wholemeal buttered toast, to serve

1 Place all ingredients into a clean
plastic food storage bag. Twist neck
and fold over and place on edge of
microwave turntable. Cook on high
1 minute.

Serve on hot toast for breakfast or
for a snack.

CHEESE, HAM AND TOMATO CROISSANT

TIME: 1 MINUTE
SERVES 1

1 croissant

2 slices cooked ham

1 small tomato, cut in wedges

1 slice cheddar cheese, halved

1 Split croissant open along centre.
Place rolled ham on bottom half and
cover with tomato wedges and sliced
cheese. Press top on securely and
wrap in clear plastic wrap.

2 Heat in microwave on defrost
1 minute.

Eat immediately for a snack or for a
tasty breakfast.

CROSTATA WITH BRIE AND ARTICHOKES

TIME: 1 MINUTE
SERVES 1

*French bread sliced obliquely,
15 cm long by 4 cm thick*

olive oil for brushing

marinated artichoke hearts

60 g (2 oz) brie cheese

pickled red capsicums (peppers)

1 Brush top of bread slice with
olive oil. Cover with wedges of
marinated artichoke hearts. Slice brie
thinly and place on top of artichokes.
Cover with strips of pickled red
pepper. Wrap up carefully in clear
plastic wrap.

2 Heat in microwave on defrost
1 to 2 minutes, until cheese starts
to soften and melt.

Serve with a side salad for a light
lunch or supper.

PARTY CHEESE BALL

TIME: 2 TO 3 MINUTES
SERVES 12 TO 14

> ¼ cup finely chopped green capsicum (pepper)
>
> ¼ cup finely chopped spring onions (shallots)
>
> 1 teaspoon butter
>
> 250 g (8 oz) cream cheese
>
> 2 cups (250 g/8 oz) grated cheddar cheese
>
> 125 g (4 oz) blue vein cheese, crumbled
>
> 1 tablespoon canned pimiento or red capsicum (pepper), chopped
>
> 2 teaspoons prepared horseradish
>
> 2 teaspoons Worcestershire sauce
>
> 1 clove garlic, very finely chopped
>
> 1 cup (125 g/4 oz) chopped pecans, walnuts or almond flakes

1 In a bowl, combine green capsicum, spring onions and butter. Cover and cook on high 45 seconds.

2 Place cream cheese in a large bowl. Cook on medium 1 to 1½ minutes or until softened. Stir in vegetables and remaining ingredients, except nuts.

3 Shape into a ball. Wrap in plastic wrap and chill 2 to 3 hours.

4 Unwrap, roll in chopped or flaked nuts and serve with assorted crackers and celery sticks.

MEXICAN NACHOS

TIME: 10½ MINUTES
SERVES 4

MEXICAN BEAN DIP

> 410 g (13 oz) can red kidney beans, drained
>
> 2 teaspoons chilli sauce
>
> freshly ground black pepper
>
> 1 green chilli, chopped
>
> 1 small onion, finely chopped

GUACAMOLE

> 1 tomato
>
> 1 large ripe avocado
>
> 1 tablespoon finely chopped onion
>
> 1 teaspoon olive oil
>
> 1 teaspoon fresh lemon juice
>
> ½ teaspoon salt
>
> freshly ground black pepper
>
> 1 clove garlic, crushed

CHIPS AND CHEESE

> 200 g (6½ oz) corn chips
>
> 2 cups grated cheddar cheese
>
> 4 tablespoons sour cream

1 Place all ingredients for Mexican Bean Dip in a food processor or a blender bowl. Chop roughly. Set aside.

2 For Guacamole, slit skin around outside of tomato and place in microwave oven. Cook on high 30 seconds. Peel tomato and chop finely. Scoop out flesh of avocado and mash. Combine tomato pulp, avocado, onion, olive oil, lemon juice, salt, pepper and garlic. Blend till smooth.

3 In each of 4 shallow serving bowls, place a quarter of the Mexican Bean Dip. Top with half the cheese, then all the corn chips and the remaining grated cheddar cheese. Cook 2 bowls at a time on high 4 to 5 minutes.

4 Spoon over 2 tablespoons of Guacamole and 1 of sour cream.

Serve hot.

PUFF PASTRY PIZZAS

TIME: 20 MINUTES
SERVES 4

> 1 sheet ready-rolled frozen puff pastry, thawed
>
> ½ (125 ml/4 fl oz) cup tomato paste
>
> 1 small onion, finely chopped
>
> 1 teaspoon dried oregano
>
> salt to taste
>
> freshly ground black pepper
>
> 4 mushrooms, sliced
>
> 1 tablespoon black olives
>
> 8 slices salami or 2 cabanosi, sliced
>
> 1 tablespoon chopped parsley
>
> 125 g (4 oz) mozzarella cheese, grated
>
> paprika

1 Cut pastry sheet into quarters. Combine tomato paste, onion, oregano, salt and pepper. Spread a quarter of the topping over each square and top with mushrooms, olives and salami. Sprinkle with parsley, mozzarella, and paprika.

2 Preheat a browning dish on high 5 minutes. Cook squares on high 15 minutes. Stand 1 minute before serving.

Serve for a hearty snack with a mug of soup.

Puff Pastry Pizzas

SALAMI WHIRLS

TIME: 20 MINUTES
MAKES 36

2 sheets ready-rolled frozen puff pastry, thawed

1 egg yolk, beaten

1 tablespoon chopped parsley

1 tablespoon sesame seeds

12 slices salami

extra sesame seeds

1 Lightly brush one side of pastry with egg yolk and sprinkle with parsley and sesame seeds.

2 Arrange salami slices on pastry then carefully roll up into a log shape. Brush with egg and sprinkle with sesame seeds.

Asparagus Omelette

3 Slice log into 5 cm (2 in) wide pieces and place flat on greaseproof paper on 2 microwave-safe platters. Cook each platter on high 8 to 10 minutes.

4 When cooked, allow to cool on a cake rack and serve warm for a snack or party savoury.

ASPARAGUS OMELETTE

TIME: 14 MINUTES
SERVES 2

1½ cups roughly chopped, fresh asparagus

2 tablespoons water

⅓ cup grated Swiss cheese

4 eggs, separated

¼ cup chopped onion

¼ cup chopped green capsicum (pepper)

4 tablespoons milk

1 teaspoon plain (all purpose) flour

¼ teaspoon salt

⅛ teaspoon white pepper

15 g (½ oz) butter

1 Place asparagus and water in a 1 litre (32 fl oz) casserole dish. Cover and cook on high 6 minutes, or until tender. Stir after 3 minutes. Drain, stir in cheese, cover and let stand.

2 Combine egg yolks, onion, capsicum, milk, flour and seasonings. Set aside. In a bowl, beat egg whites until stiff, then fold into yolk mixture.

3 Melt butter in a microwave-safe pie plate on high 1 minute or until melted. Tilt dish to coat. Pour egg mixture into buttered dish and cook on medium 7 to 10 minutes or until set, lifting edges every 2 minutes with a spatula so uncooked portion spreads evenly.

4 Top with asparagus, fold over in half and cut into wedges to serve.

Serve for breakfast or brunch.

PRAWN OMELETTES

TIME: 13 MINUTES
SERVES 5

4 eggs

250 g (8 oz) fresh mushrooms, sliced

⅓ cup finely chopped spring onions (shallots)

1 cup (60 g/2 oz) bean sprouts

⅛ teaspoon white pepper

140 g (4½ oz) prawn meat

2 tablespoons oil

1½ teaspoons cornflour

Add vegetables and prawns to beaten eggs

Pour half cup measures of mixture into dish

2 teaspoons soy sauce

2 teaspoons oyster sauce

¼ cup (60 ml/2 fl oz) chicken stock

1 teaspoon sugar

1 In a medium-sized bowl, beat eggs well. Fold in mushrooms, spring onions, bean sprouts, pepper and prawn meat. Cook on high 4 minutes, stirring 3 to 4 times until soft set.

2 Preheat browning dish on high 5 minutes, then add oil. Using a half-cup measure, pour mixture into dish

Prawn Omelettes

to make 5 small omelettes. When sizzling stops turn omelette over and cook on high 1½ minutes until firm and set. Cover and set aside.

3 In a bowl combine cornflour, soy sauce, oyster sauce, chicken stock and sugar. Cook on high 2 to 3 minutes or until thickened, stirring during cooking.

4 Pour sauce over omelettes to serve.

Serve for a light snack.

Cook omelettes on both sides until firm

For the Sweet Tooth

*F*or those with a sweet tooth, it is easy to whip something up quickly in your microwave oven. Highly organised cooks can microwave the dessert while the main course is being enjoyed! The microwave will stew and poach seasonal fruits perfectly for a speedy simple dessert. It cooks old-fashioned hot puddings, crumbcrust pies and cheesecakes. This chapter is full of delicious sweet surprises for you to enjoy.

STRAWBERRIES AND KIWIFRUIT IN CHAMPAGNE

TIME: 2 MINUTES
SERVES 6

1 sugar cube

2 cups (500 ml/16 fl oz) champagne

pinch ground nutmeg

36 strawberries, hulled and halved

3 kiwi fruit, peeled and sliced

1 Place sugar cube, champagne and nutmeg in mixing bowl. Cook on high 2 minutes. Stir.

2 Divide fruit equally between 6 parfait glasses. Pour over champagne.

Serve chilled.

MAKING STRAWBERRY FANS

Wash and hull strawberries and with a sharp, thin bladed knife make 5 to 6 cuts into each strawberry. These cuts should extend only two-thirds into the strawberry from the top. Carefully separate slices until the strawberry takes on a fan shape.

Recipes on previous pages: Apple and Berry Crumble, Lemon Delicious Pudding (page 88)

MELTING BUTTER

30 g (1 oz) butter: 30 to 45 seconds on high

125 g (4 oz) butter: 1 minute on high

250 g (8 oz): 1 to 2 minutes on high

CHOCOLATE FLAKE CHEESECAKE

TIME: 23 MINUTES
SERVES 8 TO 10

1½ cups (160 g/5 oz) semi-sweet biscuit crumbs

2 tablespoons sugar

½ teaspoon ground cinnamon

½ teaspoon ground nutmeg

90 g (3 oz) unsalted butter, melted

4 cups (1 kg/2 lb) cream-style cottage cheese

1 cup (250 ml/8 fl oz) sour cream

6 eggs, beaten

1½ cups (375 g/12 oz) sugar

½ cup (60 g/2 oz) plain (all purpose) flour

3 chocolate flake bars, crumbled

1 teaspoon rum essence

1 Combine biscuit crumbs, sugar, cinnamon, nutmeg and butter. Press mixture into base and sides of a 25 cm (10 in) ceramic flan dish. Cook on high 3 minutes. Chill till set.

2 Combine cottage cheese, sour cream, eggs and sugar. Beat thoroughly. Fold in sifted flour. Fold in 2 flake bars and rum essence. Pour mixture into biscuit crust. Cook on medium 15 to 20 minutes.

3 Stand for 10 minutes. Decorate with extra chocolate flake bar.

Serve cold accompanied with vanilla ice cream.

PAVLOVA ROLL

TIME: 3 MINUTES
SERVES 8

2 teaspoons melted butter

2 teaspoons cornflour

6 egg whites

1½ cups (375 g/12 oz) caster sugar

¾ teaspoon vanilla essence

1 teaspoon white vinegar

½ cup toasted flaked almonds

1 tablespoon cinnamon sugar

2 cups fresh strawberries

1¼ cups (300 ml/10 fl oz) cream, whipped

1 Place butter in small bowl and cook on high 15 seconds to melt. Lightly grease a 30 x 30 cm (12 x 12 in) tray and line base with greaseproof paper. Regrease and dust lightly with cornflour and shake off excess.

2 Whisk egg whites until firm peaks form. Add sugar, 1 tablespoon at a time, beating until dissolved. Fold in vanilla and vinegar.

3 Spread meringue evenly into prepared tray and sprinkle with toasted almonds. Cook on high 3 minutes and allow to cool.

4 Sprinkle a large sheet of greaseproof paper with cinnamon sugar and turn pavlova onto it. Slice 1½ cups of strawberries and fold into whipped cream. Spread cream over two-thirds of the pavlova.

5 Roll up as for a Swiss roll. Pipe rosettes of cream on top and decorate with remaining strawberries, cut into fans. Chill before serving.

Chilled Strawberry Soup

Place strawberries, sugar and water in casserole

Pour arrowroot, wine and orange juice over strawberries

Purée soup in food processor

CHILLED STRAWBERRY SOUP

TIME: 14 MINUTES
SERVES 8

> 3 cups sliced strawberries
>
> 1 cup (250 g/8 oz) sugar
>
> ½ cup (125 ml/4 fl oz) water
>
> 2 teaspoons arrowroot
>
> 2 tablespoons cold water
>
> 1 cup (250 ml/8 fl oz) red wine
>
> 1 cup (250 ml/8 fl oz) orange juice
>
> 1½ cups (375 ml/12 fl oz) sour cream
>
> strawberries, to garnish

1 Place strawberries, sugar and ½ cup water in a 2 litre (64 fl oz) casserole dish. Cover and cook on high 3 minutes or until boiling. Cook 5 minutes on medium.

2 Blend arrowroot with 2 tablespoons water, then blend with wine and orange juice into strawberry mixture. Cook on high 6 minutes or until boiling. Chill mixture.

3 Purée in food processor. Stir in sour cream and serve chilled as a dessert. Garnish with sliced strawberries.

Press biscuit mixture into base of flan dish

Use a metal spoon to fold in egg whites

Pour mixture into biscuit base

Strawberry Cheesecake

STRAWBERRY CHEESECAKE

TIME: 23 MINUTES
SERVES 8 TO 12

45 g (1½ oz) butter

125 g (4 oz) biscuit crumbs

500 g (1 lb) cream cheese, softened

½ cup (125 g/4 oz) caster sugar

2 egg yolks

1 teaspoon grated lemon zest

1 tablespoon fresh lemon juice, strained

2 stiffly beaten egg whites

TOPPING

1 cup (250 ml/8 fl oz) sour cream

1 tablespoon sugar

1 teaspoon vanilla essence

1 punnet strawberries

1 jar fruit gel or sieved strawberry jam

1 Place butter in a bowl and soften on high 1 minute. Stir in biscuit

crumbs and cook on high 2 minutes. Press crumb mixture into base of a ceramic or glass flan dish.

2 In a large bowl beat cream cheese, sugar, egg yolks, lemon zest and juice until creamy. Avoid overbeating. Fold in stiffly beaten egg whites, using a metal spoon. Pour into prepared crumbcrust and cook on defrost 20 minutes. Allow to cool.

3 In a small bowl, beat sour cream, sugar and vanilla until sugar dissolves. Spread over cheesecake.

4 Wash and dry strawberries, place on cheesecake and coat evenly with fruit gel. Chill until firm before serving.

BAKED HONEY PEARS

TIME: 8 MINUTES
SERVES 4

> 4 firm pears
> 4 tablespoons chopped dates
> 2 tablespoons chopped walnuts
> 3 tablespoons honey
> ¼ teaspoon ground cinnamon

1 Peel pears. Cut off caps 2.5 cm (1 in) from top. Core each pear without cutting right through. Remove seeds.

2 Mix dates with walnuts, honey and cinnamon. Fill pear centres with date mixture, replace caps. Arrange in a circle on a glass plate and cook on high 6 to 8 minutes.

3 Pears can be served whole; remove cap and top with whipped cream, or cut in half and serve with a rosette of whipped cream piped onto each pear half.

FRENCH CHERRY TART

TIME: 21 MINUTES
SERVES 6

> 23 cm (9 in) pastry crust (see Hazelnut Pie, page 91)
> 2 eggs
> ½ cup (125 g/4 oz) caster sugar
> 4 tablespoons ground almonds
> 2 tablespoons sour cream
> 810 g (26 oz) can pitted black cherries, drained
> ½ teaspoon ground nutmeg
> whipped cream

1 Beat together eggs, caster sugar, 2 tablespoons ground almonds and sour cream till fluffy.

2 Arrange cherries in a layer on base of pie crust. Pour over egg mixture. Sprinkle remaining almonds and nutmeg over pie. Cook on medium 15 to 20 minutes. Stand 5 minutes.

Serve with whipped cream.

MELTING CHOCOLATE

When melting chocolate test it with a skewer or plastic spoon to confirm that it has in fact melted, and not just softened. When reheating melted or softened chocolate be careful to avoid burning.

PEARS WITH CHOCOLATE SAUCE

TIME: 14 MINUTES
SERVES 6

> 6 firm pears
> 1 tablespoon fresh lemon juice, strained
> ¼ cup (60 g/2 oz) sugar
> 2 tablespoons dry sherry
> 2 tablespoons Grand Marnier
> 180 g (6 oz) cooking chocolate
> 45 g (1½ oz) unsalted butter
> custard sauce, optional

1 Peel pears, leaving stems intact. De-core from the base by cutting a circle with a paring knife or use an apple corer. Brush with lemon juice to prevent discolouring.

2 In a 1 litre (32 fl oz) casserole combine sugar, sherry and Grand Marnier. Place pears on sides with the thicker ends towards the outside. Add remaining lemon juice and cover. Cook on high 6 minutes. Turn pears over and baste. Cover and cook a further 6 minutes or until tender. Remove pears. Reserve poaching liquid.

3 Measure ½ cup poaching liquid and return to casserole. Add cooking chocolate in pieces and cook on medium 2 minutes or until melted. Add butter and whisk till smooth.

4 Fill each pear with custard sauce, if desired. Place upright on serving dish. Pour remaining custard around pears and spoon chocolate sauce over top.

APPLE AND BERRY CRUMBLE

TIME: 11 MINUTES
SERVES 4

> 500 g (1 lb) green cooking apples
>
> 250 g (8 oz) berries —
> strawberries, blackberries or
> boysenberries
>
> 3 tablespoons raw sugar
>
> 1 tablespoon water

CRUMBLE

> ½ cup (60 g/2 oz) wholemeal
> plain (all purpose) flour
>
> 60 g (2 oz) unsalted butter,
> cubed
>
> ½ cup (100 g/3½ oz) toasted
> muesli
>
> ¼ teaspoon ground nutmeg
>
> ¼ teaspoon ground cloves
>
> 2 tablespoons raw sugar

1 Peel, core and slice apples into a ceramic pie dish or soufflé dish. Stir in berries and sugar. Add water. Cover with clear plastic wrap and cook on high 5 minutes or until apple is tender.

2 Place flour and butter in a food processor and mix for 30 seconds. Transfer to a bowl and stir in remaining ingredients. Sprinkle crumble topping over fruit and cook in microwave oven on medium 6 minutes or until cooked.

Serve warm with cream, ice cream or custard sauce.

PRESERVED BERRIES

Canned berries may be used in place of fresh berries if berries are not in season.

LEMON DELICIOUS PUDDING

TIME: 7 MINUTES
SERVES 4

> 1 cup (250 g/8 oz) caster sugar
>
> ¼ cup (30 g/1 oz) plain (all
> purpose) flour
>
> finely grated rind of 1 large
> lemon
>
> ¼ cup (60 ml/2 fl oz) fresh
> lemon juice
>
> 60 g (2 oz) unsalted butter,
> melted
>
> 3 eggs, separated
>
> 1½ cups (375 ml/12 fl oz) milk

1 Place half the sugar, the flour, lemon rind and juice, melted butter and egg yolks into a mixing bowl and beat until well mixed.

2 Heat milk on medium 1 minute until lukewarm and stir into mixture.

3 Whisk egg whites until stiff, then whisk in remaining sugar quickly. Fold egg whites into lemon mixture. Pour into a soufflé dish and cook on high for 5 minutes, then on medium 2 minutes or until cooked.

Serve warm.

CHOCOLATE NUT ICE CREAM CAKE

TIME: 25 MINUTES
SERVES 10 TO 12

CAKE

> 250 g (8 oz) flaked almonds
>
> 1 packet chocolate cake mix
>
> 60 g (2 oz) unsalted butter,
> melted
>
> 2 eggs
>
> ½ cup (125 ml/4 fl oz) milk
>
> 1 tablespoon rum

ICE CREAM

> 6 egg yolks, beaten
>
> 2 cups (500 g/1 lb) sugar
>
> 100 g (3 oz) milk chocolate
>
> 1¾ cups (300 g/9 oz) icing sugar
>
> 1 tablespoon drinking chocolate
>
> 4 x 300 ml (10 fl oz) cartons
> cream, whipped

GARNISH (OPTIONAL)

> 4 strawberries
>
> 1 kiwi fruit, peeled and sliced
>
> 2 tablespoons cherry brandy or
> brandy

1 Combine flaked almonds, chocolate cake mix, butter, 2 eggs and milk. Blend together till smooth. Pour batter into a 23 cm (9 in) cake dish. Cook on medium 15 minutes. Stand 10 minutes, uncovered.

2 Crumble cake, add rum to crumbs. Set aside.

3 Combine egg yolks and sugar in a 2 litre (64 fl oz) casserole dish. Cook on medium 5 to 7 minutes. Stir twice. Set aside. Break up chocolate into a glass jug. Melt on medium 2 to 3 minutes. Stir.

4 Sift together icing sugar and drinking chocolate. Fold together egg yolk mixture, melted chocolate, icing sugar, drinking chocolate and cream. Blend evenly.

5 Press 1 cup cake crumble into a 20 cm (8 in) spring-form cake tin, then pour over 2 cups ice cream mix. Repeat layering ¾ cup crumble and 2 cups ice cream finishing with ice cream. Freeze for 6 to 8 hours.

6 One hour before serving, carefully release spring-form tin. Mark surface of cake into slices. Decorate with strawberries and kiwi fruit. Freeze for 1 hour.

Pour over cherry brandy and serve immediately.

CHOCOLATE SAUCE

TIME: 4 MINUTES

SERVES 4

  6 teaspoons cornflour

  2 tablespoons cocoa

  1¼ cups (300 ml/10 fl oz) milk

  75 g (2½ oz) sugar

  1 teaspoon butter

1 Blend cornflour and cocoa with 3 tablespoons milk. Place remaining milk into a jug and cook 2 minutes to boil. Blend in cornflour mixture and cook 2 minutes. Blend in sugar and butter.

Serve Chocolate Sauce with profiteroles or cream puffs, crepes or ice cream.

Chocolate Sauce

PECAN CHOCOLATE CAKE

TIME: 19½ MINUTES
SERVES 8

125 g (4 oz) unsalted butter

⅔ cup (125 g/4 oz) brown sugar

⅔ cup (60 g/2 oz) coconut

⅔ cup (100 g/3 oz) chopped pecans

1½ cups (185 g/6 oz) plain (all purpose) flour

1⅓ cups (325 g/11 oz) caster sugar

¼ cup (30 g/1 oz) cocoa

1½ teaspoons baking powder

1 teaspoon salt

1 cup (250 ml/8 fl oz) milk

160 g (5½ oz) unsalted butter, extra

3 eggs

1 teaspoon vanilla essence

1 Line base of 2 x 23 cm (9 in) soufflé dishes with two rounds of greaseproof paper. Place butter in a bowl and cook on high 1½ minutes. Stir in brown sugar, coconut and pecans. Spread mixture evenly over base of each dish and set aside.

2 Place remaining ingredients in a mixing bowl. Blend at low speed. Beat 2 minutes on medium then divide mixture and spread evenly in each dish.

3 Cook one cake at a time on medium 6 minutes then increase to high and cook 2 to 3 minutes until cake is light and spongy to touch. Let stand 5 minutes.

4 Turn one cake onto serving plate. Turn second cake out onto the topping side of the first cake.

MINT SLICE

TIME: 1½ MINUTES
MAKES 25

180 g (6 oz) cooking chocolate

45 g (1½ oz) unsalted butter

1 cup (155 g/5 oz) icing sugar

⅛ teaspoon peppermint essence

3 to 5 drops green food colouring

3 to 4 teaspoons milk

1 Cut chocolate into small cubes and combine with 30 g (1 oz) butter in a small bowl. Cook on high 1 to 1½ minutes or until chocolate is soft to touch. Stir until smooth. Spread in a 20 x 20 cm (8 x 8 in) square dish and chill until set.

2 In a medium-sized bowl combine icing sugar, 15 g (½ oz) butter, peppermint essence, green food colouring and milk. Beat with electric hand mixer until smooth. Spread over chilled chocolate and refrigerate until firm.

3 Cut into squares. Store, covered, in refrigerator.

THICKER MINT SLICE BASE

Double the amount of chocolate and butter used in the base.

Pecan Chocolate Cake

Line pie plate with pastry and chill

Combine filling ingredients

Pour cooked filling into pastry crust

Hazelnut Pie

HAZELNUT PIE

TIME: 18 MINUTES
SERVES 6 TO 8

PASTRY

> 1 cup (125 g/4 oz) plain (all purpose) flour
>
> 125 g (4 oz) unsalted butter
>
> 3 tablespoons cold water

FILLING

> 3 eggs
>
> ½ cup (90 g/3 oz) brown sugar
>
> 1 cup (250 ml/8 fl oz) corn syrup
>
> 30 g (1 oz) unsalted butter
>
> 1 tablespoon plain (all purpose) flour
>
> 1 teaspoon vanilla essence
>
> 1 cup roughly chopped roasted hazelnuts

1 To make pastry, sieve flour into a medium-sized bowl. Cut in butter to resemble coarse crumbs. Blend in water and knead lightly. Let rest in refrigerator 15 minutes. Roll out, line a 23 cm (9 in) china pie plate and chill a further 10 minutes.

2 Beat 1 egg yolk lightly and brush evenly over prepared pastry case to seal. Cook on high 45 seconds until yolk has set.

3 In a mixing bowl, combine remaining eggs with separated white and leftover beaten yolk. Add remaining ingredients, except hazelnuts. Blend well. Stir in hazelnuts and cook on high 4 minutes, stirring after 2 minutes.

4 Pour into pastry case. Reduce power to medium and cook 10 to 13 minutes until filling has almost set. Let stand 6 minutes before serving. The standing time completes the cooking.

Serve hot or cold with whipped cream.

MANGO GINGERBREAD

TIME: 13 TO 16 MINUTES

60 g (2 oz) unsalted butter
½ cup (90 g/3 oz) brown sugar
1 tablespoon milk
2 cups peeled, sliced fresh mango
1 packet gingerbread mix

1 Cook butter on high 1 to 1½ minutes in a 20 x 20 cm (8 x 8 in) square dish. Blend in sugar and milk and cook on high 2 minutes, stirring twice.

2 Arrange mango slices in rows on top. Prepare gingerbread as directed on package. Spoon batter evenly over fruit and cook on medium 6 minutes.

3 Increase power to high and cook 4 to 6 minutes until gingerbread springs back when touched. Cool 5 minutes. Loosen edges and turn out onto platter.

Cut into slices or squares. If desired, top with whipped cream or ice cream to serve.

MARASCHINO CHOCOLATE CLUSTERS

TIME: 3 MINUTES
MAKES 24

200 g (6½ oz) dark cooking chocolate

30 g (1 oz) unsalted butter
1 teaspoon maraschino cherry juice
90 g (3 oz) maraschino cherries, chopped
60 g (2 oz) almond slivers

1 Break chocolate into pieces. Place chocolate, butter and maraschino juice in mixing bowl and cook on high 2 to 3 minutes. Stir.

2 Fold through chopped cherries and almond slivers. Spoon into small paper cases and allow to set.

Serve with after-dinner coffee.

Mango Gingerbread

CHOCOLATE TRUFFLES

TIME: 4 MINUTES
MAKES 18 TO 22 BALLS

300 g (10 oz) milk cooking chocolate

150 g (5 oz) unsalted butter

1 tablespoon rum

¼ cup (60 ml/2 fl oz) sour cream

extra 60 g (2 oz) chocolate, grated or chocolate sprinkles

1 Break up chocolate. Place butter, chocolate and rum into a 2 litre (64 fl oz) mixing bowl. Cook on high 3 to 4 minutes. Stir to melt chocolate.

2 Fold in sour cream. Pour mixture into shallow dish. Allow to chill for 1 hour in refrigerator.

3 Quickly spoon 1 teaspoon of mixture onto grated chocolate, working to form a ball. Coat with extra grated chocolate or chocolate sprinkles. Chill till set.

Serve with after-dinner coffee.

Chocolate Truffles

CARROT CAKE

TIME: 9 MINUTES

125 g (4 oz) unsalted butter or margarine

½ cup (90 g/3 oz) firmly packed brown sugar

1 egg

1 cup firmly packed grated carrot

1 tablespoon crystallised ginger

½ cup seeded raisins

½ cup sultanas

1½ cups (185 g/6 oz) double sifted plain (all purpose) flour

1 teaspoon baking powder

½ teaspoon bicarbonate of soda

½ teaspoon ground cinnamon

½ teaspoon ground nutmeg

¾ cup (180 ml/6 fl oz) milk

FROSTING

1½ cups (250 g/8 oz) icing sugar, sifted

90 g (3 oz) cream cheese

45 g (1½ oz) unsalted butter

1 teaspoon vanilla

1 tablespoon fresh lemon juice

1 Cream butter or margarine and brown sugar. Beat in egg until well blended.

2 Stir in carrot, ginger, raisins and sultanas. Sift together flour, baking powder, bicarbonate of soda, cinnamon and nutmeg. Stir into the mixture with milk. Blend well.

3 Turn into a well greased microwave-safe ring dish and cook in oven 6 minutes on high and 3 minutes on medium.

4 To make frosting, beat all ingredients until fluffy, and spread over cake. Decorate with mandarin segments if desired.

Serve cold with lemon frosting, or hot with lemon sauce.

TO SOFTEN CREAM CHEESE

To warm: Remove foil wrapper from 125 g (4 oz) cream cheese and cut into quarters. Place in bowl and cook on medium 45 seconds.

To melt: Remove foil wrapper from 250 g (8 oz) cream cheese and cut into eighths. Place in bowl and cook on medium 1 to 1½ minutes.

Index

Apple and berry crumble 88
Asian chicken with apricots 40
Asparagus
    macadamia pasta sauce 68
    omelette 80
    sauce 14

Baby buttered potatoes 16
Baby squash provencal 17
Bagel, salami and pickle 74
Baked honey pears 87
Barbecue drumsticks 46
Beef
    see also Mince
    filet mignon, with
      mushroom sauce 51
    fillet Wellington 50
    marinated 53
Beetroot
    borscht 22
    with dill sauce 14
Borscht 22
Bouquet garni 22
Bream with chilli ginger
    sauce 35
Brie
    and artichoke crostata 77
    and smoked salmon flan 34
Broccoli
    and pasta salad 68
    salad 12
Brown rice 70
    saffron 70
Burgers, lamb 53

Cabbage, braised red 19
Cake
    carrot 93
    chocolate nut ice cream 88
    pecan chocolate 90
Calamari pasta sauce 67
Calf liver and bacon, with
    mustard cream 61
Cappuccino 74
Carrots
    cake 93
    honey glazed 14
Cashews, piri piri 76
Celery and almond sauté 14
Cheese
    ball 78
    ham and tomato
      croissant 77

and ham loaf 75
    pumpkin ring 19
Cheesecake
    chocolate flake 84
    strawberry 86
Cherry
    chocolate clusters 92
    tart 87
Chicken breasts
    with apricots 40
    and avocado salad 44
    in bacon 42
    Fijian 45
    Florentine style 41
    roulade, with almond and
      broccoli stuffing 42
    tasty Thai 40
Chicken drumsticks
    orange pecan 46
    tangy barbecue 46
Chicken thighs
    coq au vin 40
    dijonnaise 42
    and eggplant cacciatore 44
Chicken, whole
    crab stuffed 43
    in spicy sauce 43
Chicken wings, Mexican
    salsa 46
Chilled strawberry soup 84
Chilli ginger sauce 35
Chinese ravioli 64
Chocolate
    flake cheesecake 84
    hot mocha 74
    maraschino clusters 92
    nut ice cream cake 88
    pecan cake 90
    sauce 87, 89
    thick shake 74
    truffles 93
Chow mein, turkey 68
Coconut
    milk 11
    prawn cutlets, with curry
      sauce 28
Cod, curried 36
Coffee
    cappuccino 74
    hot mocha chocolate 74
    Irish 74
Coq au vin 40
Coriander pesto 67
Crab
    mousse 31
    stuffed chicken 43
    stuffed flounder fillets 33

Crayfish with lemon butter
    sauce 31
Croissant, cheese, ham and
    tomato 77
Crostata with brie and
    artichokes 77
Crumble, apple and berry 88
Curry
    sauce 28
    smoked cod supreme 36

Dill sauce 14
Dipping sauce 76
Dressing 13
    Italian 12
    vinaigrette 13

Eggs
    see also Omelettes
    en cocotte 77

Felafel bean roll 75
Fettuccine
    with calamari sauce 67
    carbonara 64
Fijian chicken 45
Filet mignon with mushroom
    sauce 51
Fish stock 36
Fish with orange coriander
    sauce 32
Flan *see* Tart
Flounder fillets, stuffed with
    crab 33
French cherry tart 87
Frosting 93

Gado gado salad 11
Gazpacho 21
Gingerbread, mango 92
Golden nugget pumpkins,
    stuffed 16
Green and white salad 13

Hazelnut pie 91
Herring rollmops 32
Hollandaise sauce 58
Honey
    glazed carrots 14
    pears 87
    sauce 14
Hot mocha chocolate 74

Ice cream chocolate nut
    cake 88
Irish coffee 74
Italian dressing 12

Jacket potatoes 16
Jewfish cutlets with creamy
    sauce 33

Lamb
    burgers 53
    lemon saté 53
    racks, with minty mustard
      topping 54
Lasagne
    savory 67
    vegetable 18
Lemon
    butter 31
    delicious pudding 88
    lamb saté 53
    rice 70
Liver and bacon with mustard
    cream 61

Magic mince 59
Mango gingerbread 92
Maraschino chocolate
    clusters 92
Marinated beef 53
Mexican nachos 78
Mexican pizza 76
Mexican salsa chicken 46
Mexican tacos 60
Mince
    magic 59
    Mexican tacos 60
Minestrone 22
Mint slice 90
Mocha chocolate 74
Mousse, crab 31
Mushrooms
    sauce 51
    on toast 77
Mussels, stuffed 30
Mustard
    cream 61
    homemade 53

Nachos, Mexican 78
Noodles, seafood 76

Omelettes
    asparagus 80
    prawn 80
Orange
    coriander sauce 32
    pecan drumsticks 46
Oysters kilpatrick 28

Parsley rice ring 71
Party cheese ball 78

ENJOY A WORLD OF GOOD COOKING WITH THE
BAY BOOKS COOKERY COLLECTION

   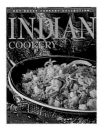

   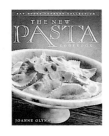

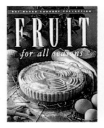 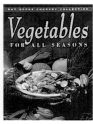   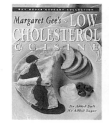  

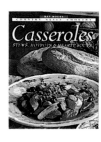    

If these titles are not available from your regular stockists, please contact the HarperCollins Sales Office in your State:

WESTERN AUSTRALIA	SOUTH AUSTRALIA	QUEENSLAND	VICTORIA	NEW SOUTH WALES
SUITE 2 , 25 BELGRAVIA ST	UNIT 1 , 1-7 UNION ST	643 KESSELS ROAD	22-24 JOSEPH STREET	25 RYDE ROAD
BELMONT WA 6104	STEPNEY SA 5069	UPPER MOUNT GRAVATT	NORTH BLACKBURN	PYMBLE NSW 2073
TEL: (09) 479 4988	TEL: (08) 363 0122	QLD 4122	VIC 3130	TEL: (02) 952 5000
FAX: (09) 478 3248	FAX: (08) 363 1653	TEL: (07) 849 7855	TEL: (03) 895 8100	FAX: (02) 952 5777
		FAX: (07) 349 8286	FAX: (03) 895 8199	